# VISUAL DICTIONARY

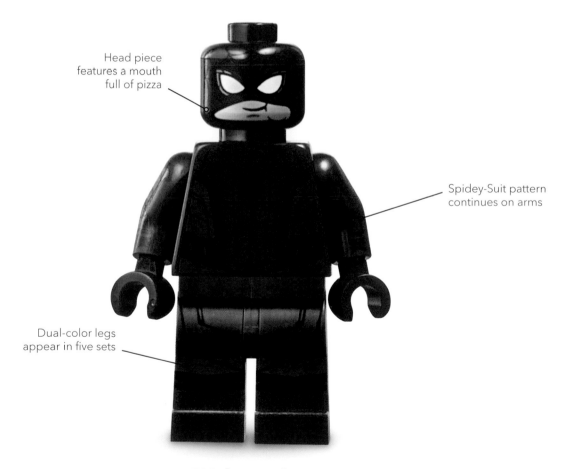

Head piece features a mouth full of pizza

Spidey-Suit pattern continues on arms

Dual-color legs appear in five sets

Written by

Simon Hugo and Amy Richau

# CONTENTS

## Chapter Three
## GUARDIANS OF THE GALAXY AND OTHER TEAMS

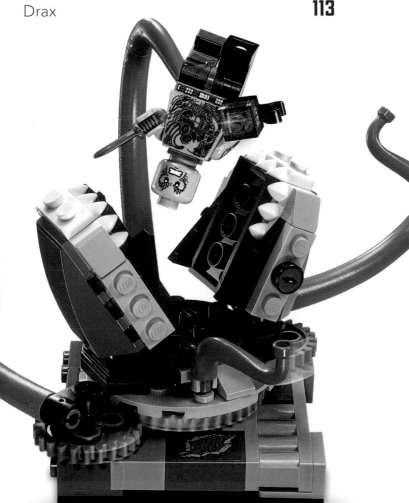

## Chapter Four
## SPECIAL SETS

## Chapter Five
## BEHIND THE SCENES

# INTRODUCTION

The LEGO Group has been turning Super Heroes and Super Villains into brick form since 2012. Prepare to be amazed by the rich detail in each and every LEGO® set, all packed full of characters, vehicles, creatures, buildings, and accessories from the Marvel Cinematic Universe (MCU) and Marvel Comics.

Get a close-up look at movie-accurate details, from Iron Man's helmet to the glorious architecture of Doctor Strange's Sanctum Sanctorum. Spot the differences between MCU and Marvel Comics minifigures, and delight in how creatively the LEGO Designers have brought them to life.

—— New York fire hydrant

## ⊙ GRAY BOXES

To make sure no one gets confused between the world of the MCU and the many worlds of Marvel Comics, this book keeps them separate. Gray boxes like this one let you know that the LEGO set depicts a non-MCU storyline. While S.H.I.E.L.D.'s Agent Coulson and his cool car *do* appear in the MCU, this set has him facing off against Justin Hammer's Detroit Steel armor—an adventure from the pages of Marvel Comics.

Agent Coulson calls his red Corvette Lola

## BRICK FACTS

These little boxes point out fascinating LEGO details, such as moving parts, transformable vehicles, or playful set features.

| Set name | Iron Man: Detroit Steel Strikes | |
|---|---|---|
| **Number** 76077 | | **Pieces** 377 |
| **Year** 2017 | | **Characters** 3 |

'Characters' includes all the minifigures, big figures, and non-minifigure figures that come with a set

## MINIFIGURES

Discover facts galore about minifigures—from rare or unusual variants and new print details to unique features and amazing accessories.

No matter whether you want to take a peek at Peter Parker's *Daily Bugle* office, visit Shuri's Wakandan lab, build Thor's hammer, or pilot Star-Lord's spaceship, you will find them all here. Discover which set is the largest, which builds use LEGO elements in surprising ways, and see if you can figure out which minifigure appears in more sets than any other.

It's time to unite your heroes, assemble your LEGO bricks, and dive into the ever-changing Multiverse of LEGO® Marvel!

*Daily Bugle* tower is four stories high

# YEAR BY YEAR

Zip up your Time Suit for a time travel tour of the LEGO® Marvel Multiverse—including key sets from each year and the movies that inspired them.

## 2008

The Marvel Cinematic Universe (MCU) is born, as Marvel Studios' *Iron Man* and *The Incredible Hulk* debut in movie theaters.

## 2010

Marvel Studios' *Iron Man 2* is released in cinemas.

## 2011

Marvel Studios' *Thor* premieres, along with *Captain America: The First Avenger*.

## 2012

*Marvel's The Avengers* breaks box office records and the LEGO Marvel Super Heroes theme launches. The X-Men's Phoenix is the first of many event-exclusive minifigures and sets.

Iron Man (set 4529)

Captain America's Avenging Cycle (set 6865)

Wolverine's Chopper Showdown (set 6866)

Spider-Man's Doc Ock Ambush (set 6873)

Phoenix (set COMCON021)

## 2013

Marvel Studios' *Iron Man 3* blasts onto the big screen, followed by *Thor: The Dark World*. The year's LEGO Marvel sets focus on Spider-Man and Iron Man.

Spider-Man: Spider-Cycle Chase (set 76004)

Spider-Man: Daily Bugle Showdown (set 76005)

Iron Man: Extremis Sea Port Battle (set 76006)

Iron Man: Malibu Mansion Attack (set 76007)

## 2014

Marvel Studios' *Captain America: The Winter Soldier* hits theaters and *Guardians of the Galaxy* takes the MCU into outer space, inspiring three LEGO Marvel sets.

Spider-Helicopter Rescue (set 76016)

Avengers: Captain America Vs. Hydra (set 76017)

The Milano Spaceship Rescue (set 76021)

X-Men Vs. The Sentinel (set 76022)

Marvel Studios' *Avengers: Age of Ultron* and *Ant-Man* are this year's blockbusters, with LEGO sets based on both. The S.H.I.E.L.D. Helicarrier launches as the biggest-ever LEGO Marvel set.

Marvel Studios' *Captain America: Civil War* and *Doctor Strange* make magic on the big screen, while Mighty Micros sets put a fresh spin on LEGO Marvel Super Heroes.

Marvel Studios' *Guardians of the Galaxy Vol. 2*, *Spider-Man: Homecoming*, and *Thor: Ragnarok* take the MCU in new directions, each featuring in at least one LEGO set.

Marvel Studios' *Black Panther*, *Avengers: Infinity War*, and *Ant-Man and The Wasp* thrill moviegoers, while The Hulkbuster: Ultron Edition celebrates 10 years of the MCU.

The Avengers Quinjet City Chase (set 76032)

Black Panther Pursuit (set 76047)

Captain America Jet Pursuit (set 76076)

Royal Talon Fighter Attack (set 76100)

Rhino and Sandman Super Villain Team-Up (set 76037)

Avenjet Space Mission (set 76049)

Ayesha's Revenge (set 76080)

Thor's Weapon Quest (set 76102)

Ant-Man Final Battle (set 76039)

Spider-Man: Web Warriors Ultimate Bridge Battle (set 76057)

ATM Heist Battle (set 76082)

The Hulkbuster: Ultron Edition (set 76105)

The Hydra Fortress Smash (set 76041)

Doctor Strange's Sanctum Sanctorum (set 76060)

The Ultimate Battle for Asgard (set 76084)

Quantum Realm Explorers (set 76109)

The S.H.I.E.L.D. Helicarrier (set 76042)

Mighty Micros: Captain America Vs. Red Skull (set 76065)

Marvel Studios' *Captain Marvel*, *Avengers: Endgame* and *Spider-Man: Far from Home* conclude the big-screen Infinity Saga, as Juniors sets bring LEGO Marvel to younger builders.

Spider-Man Car Chase (set 76133)

Iron Man Helmet (set 76165)

Daily Bugle (set 76178)

Spider-Man's Spider Crawler (set 76114)

**2020**

A range of LEGO Marvel mechs introduces robot walkers for key characters, while Iron Man Helmet becomes the first LEGO Marvel bust.

Avengers Tower Battle (set 76166)

Spider-Man at the Sanctum Workshop (set 76185)

Captain Marvel and The Skrull Attack (set 76127)

Avengers Speeder Bike Attack (set 76142)

**2021**

Marvel Studios' *Black Widow*, *Shang-Chi and The Legend of The Ten Rings*, *Eternals*, and *Spider-Man: No Way Home* expand the MCU further than ever before, LEGO® Marvel Collectible Minifigures hit store shelves, and Daily Bugle becomes the biggest LEGO Marvel set.

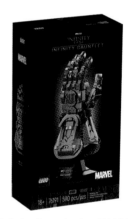

Infinity Gauntlet (set 76191)

Hydro-Man Attack (set 76129)

Spider-Man Mech (set 76146)

Rise of the Domo (set 76156)

The Avengers Advent Calendar (set 76196)

Avengers Compound Battle (set 76131)

Black Widow's Helicopter Chase (set 76162)

Escape from The Ten Rings (set 76176)

LEGO® Minifigures Marvel Studios (set 71031)

Marvel Studios' *Doctor Strange in the Multiverse of Madness*, *Thor: Love and Thunder*, and *Black Panther: Wakanda Forever* pack movie theaters, younger builders enjoy Spidey and His Amazing Friends sets, and a new Hulkbuster takes the biggest-set top spot!

King Namor's Throne Room
(set 76213)

Ant-Man Construction Figure
(set 76256)

Gargantos Showdown
(set 76205)

I am Groot (set 76217)

The New Guardians' Ship
(set 76255)

Iron Man Figure (set 76206)

Miles Morales: Spider-Man's
Techno Trike (set 10781)

The Hulkbuster: The Battle of
Wakanda (set 76247)

Marvel Studios' *Ant-Man and The Wasp: Quantumania* and *Guardians of the Galaxy Vol. 3* light up the silver screen, with LEGO Marvel sets based on all three movies—and more besides!

The Goat Boat (set 76208)

The Avengers Quinjet
(set 76248)

Hulkbuster (set 76210)

Miles Morales Vs. Morbius
(set 76244)

Star-Lord's Helmet (set 76251)

**Infinity Gauntlet**

# Chapter 1:
# SPIDER-MAN

# SPIDER-MAN

As a smart, science-loving high-school student, Peter Parker was always destined for great things. But it takes a bite from a spider to turn him into one of the world's greatest Super Heroes! Peter's spiderlike powers include gravity-defying wall-climbing skills and a tingling sixth sense that warns him whenever danger is near. His high-tech Spider-Man suits, meanwhile, are fitted with web-slinging shooters that are just what he needs to swing between buildings and ensnare enemies!

**Peter can hide** his spider-suit underneath ordinary clothes. Sometimes he gets changed as he swings into action! This minifigure reveals the Spidey-Suit poking out from behind Peter's shirt.

Super-strong webbing on side of bank

Spidey shoots a web from his hand

Hulk mask obscures this criminal's face

## ▶ LOCAL HERO

When he gets his powers, Peter starts foiling crimes and doing other good deeds in the area of New York where he grew up. In this set, he halts a robbery by two armed criminals using just his sticky webbing! Spidey's heroics soon attract the attention of Iron Man, who invites him to join the Avengers. But Peter says no, choosing to remain a friendly neighborhood Spider-Man instead.

This cheeky crook is wearing a Captain America mask!

| Set name | ATM Heist Battle | |
| --- | --- | --- |
| **Number** 76082 | | **Pieces** 185 |
| **Year** 2017 | | **Minifigures** 3 |

# WORLDWIDE WEB-SLINGER

Spider-Man officially joins the Avengers when they step up to fight against the mighty warlord Thanos, who wants to take out half of the population of the universe. Spidey fights bravely, but he gets blipped out of existence for five whole years! When he returns to reality, Spider-Man finds new allies and enemies in Europe, where he battles Mysterio, who uses an army of drones to project the illusion of creatures wreaking havoc in Venice, Prague, and in the skies over London's Tower Bridge.

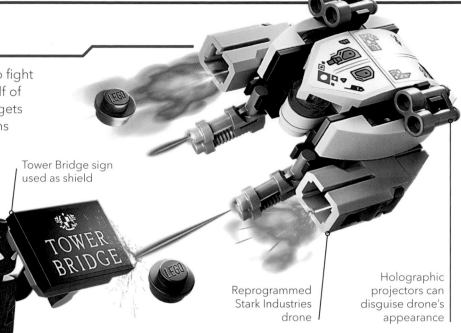

Tower Bridge sign used as shield

Upgraded red-and-black spider-suit

| Set name | Spider-Man Bridge Battle | |
|---|---|---|
| Number | 30443 | Pieces 45 |
| Year | 2022 | Minifigures 1 |

Reprogrammed Stark Industries drone

Holographic projectors can disguise drone's appearance

## MULTIVERSE MAYHEM

When the news turns the public against Spider-Man, he asks Doctor Strange for help. Strange casts a spell to make everyone forget about Spider-Man, but Peter interrupts it, causing interdimensional chaos. Spidey learns that anything can happen when you mess with The Multiverse!

Spidey shoots his webs at Strange

Strange's Sanctum Sanctorum basement is full of stuff

| Set name | Spider-Man at the Sanctum Workshop | |
|---|---|---|
| Number | 76185 | Pieces 355 |
| Year | 2022 | Minifigures 4 |

Strange isn't happy about Peter's interference!

**The advanced** Iron Spider suit was built by Tony Stark as a gift. It gives Spidey a total of eight limbs. The extra limbs attach around the minifigure's neck.

**Spidey's** integrated suit combines the best tech from the Iron Spider armor with the advanced outfit he wears at Tower Bridge.

### BRICK FACTS

There are more than 25 different Peter Parker Spider-Man minifigure designs, including a chewing-on-a-mouthful-of-pizza version!

# PETER'S FRIENDS AND FAMILY

It's not easy being Spider-Man! Luckily, Peter Parker has a host of loved ones he can rely on to get him through the tougher times. Some of them know his secret identity, making for a rare and special bond. Others, however, are blissfully unaware, meaning that Peter can hang out with them like an everyday teenager. Peter's closest relative is his beloved aunt, May, but every one of his BFFs is part of the Spider-fam.

**Happy Hogan**, a Stark Industries exec, finds Peter a little annoying at first. But he comes to admire his good heart, his heroism, and his aunt, May!

##  MJ

Just like Peter, MJ is a super smart student at New York's Midtown School of Science and Technology. It doesn't take her long to figure out that Peter is Spider-Man, and they team up to defeat the villain Mysterio—becoming boyfriend and girlfriend along the way! Sadly, a magic spell makes MJ forget all about Peter not long after.

| Set name Spider-Man at the Sanctum Workshop | |
|---|---|
| **Number** 76185 | **Pieces** 355 |
| **Year** 2022 | **Minifigures** 4 |

Determined expression

Candelabra from the Sanctum Sanctorum makes a useful weapon

Ned always has a smile for Spidey

## ◄ NED LEEDS

Ned had no idea about his best friend's secret identity—until Peter came swinging home through his bedroom window to find Ned building a LEGO® set! He then set out to become Spidey's backroom brains as well as his closest confidante, but—like MJ—lost all memory of Peter after an adventure involving The Multiverse.

| Set name Spider-Man and the Museum Break-In | |
|---|---|
| **Number** 40343 | **Pieces** 49 |
| **Year** 2019 | **Minifigures** 3 |

Spidey must hide his love for Aunt May from his enemies

Super-strong webbing can carry May's weight

This version of May is an older woman

## ◀ MAY PARKER

Peter Parker's Multiverse adventures see him meeting alternative versions of himself—and each one has his own Aunt May! Some versions of May are older than others, and some have no idea that Parker is a Super Hero. But in every reality, one thing never changes: Aunt May is the woman who raised Peter from an early age, bringing him up to be kind and conscientious.

| Set name Spider-Man: Web Warriors: Ultimate Bridge Battle | |
| --- | --- |
| Number 76057 | Pieces 1,092 |
| Year 2016 | Minifigures 7 |

**There is another MJ** in the Spider-Verse and she also knows Peter's secret identity. It's clear from the clothing her minifigure wears where her heart lies.

**Science whiz** Gwen Stacy loves Peter Parker, but she doesn't like Spider-Man! As a result, their relationship never finds a happy ending.

## ▼ THE STACY FAMILY

Peter gets to know the Stacy family when he falls in love with his college classmate Gwen Stacy. He goes on to become friends with her father too. Police Captain George Stacy deeply admires Spider-Man and helps him on several crime-fighting missions. Peter does his best to keep the Stacys from learning his secret identity, for their own safety. In this set, Captain Stacy joins Spider-Man in a rescue mission. His police boat can pull Spider-Man's web surfboard over the waves!

Captain Stacy enjoys adventure

Spidey's surfboard attaches here with rope

Stud shooter

| Set name Spider-Man: Doc Ock's Tentacle Trap | |
| --- | --- |
| Number 76059 | Pieces 446 |
| Year 2016 | Minifigures 5 |

POLICE 77

Sticker identifies boat as a police vessel

# MILES MORALES: SPIDER-MAN

When villainous scientists try to recreate Peter Parker's powers, they create a new generation of radioactive spiders. One bites teenager Miles Gonzalo Morales, and a new Spider-Man is born! He has all the same powers as Peter, but with added camouflage abilities and "venom strike" energy that blasts out of his hands. When Peter turns his attention to missions all around the world, Miles steps in to become New York's friendly neighborhood Spider-Man.

Venom strike power is bad news for enemies

## ▶ PARALLEL PARTNERS

Miles was born in a parallel world known as Earth-1610, but comes to live in the same reality as Peter Parker. Now the pair can team up to take on threats that are too big for just one Spider-Man! When alien symbiote Carnage attacks a power station, the two Spider-Men make an unmatched tag team. This set includes plenty of web accessories to help catch Carnage, including a pair of web-fluid handcuffs that are sure to come in handy.

Overloading power cells

| Set name Spider-Man Bike Rescue | |
|---|---|
| Number 76113 | Pieces 235 |
| Year 2018 | Minifigures 3 |

Carnage's long tentacles can be unpredictable

Miles leads the charge against Carnage

| Set name | Miles Morales Vs. Morbius | |
|---|---|---|
| Number | 76244 | Pieces 220 |
| Year | 2023 | Minifigures 2 |

Bats fly in
Morbius's wake

Flask full of
bats' blood

**Miles's minifigure**
wears a black
spider-suit. It is
made for him by
S.H.I.E.L.D. and
is fitted with some
of Peter Parker's
old web-shooters.

Blasters fire
electrical energy

## ⊘ SPIDER-CAR

Just like his high-tech spider-suit, Miles Morales's
Spider-Car is sleekly styled in red and black. He drives
it during a close encounter with another crimson-clad
minifigure, Morbius, the Living Vampire. There's nothing
this fanged fiend would like more than to take a bite
out of Miles, whose radioactive blood has all kinds
of special powers.

Spider fangs on
front bumper

## GOOD IN A HOOD

Even Super Heroes can
get cold! That's why Miles
sometimes wears a warming
zip-up hoodie over his
skin-tight spider-suit.

**As part of** his medical
research, Dr. Michael
Morbius injects himself
with vampire bat
DNA, becoming a
bloodsucking monster
with scarily pale skin
and red eyes!

# WEB-WARRIORS

Spider-Man isn't the only web-slinging, wall-crawling hero. In his own world, he is joined by the likes of Spider-Girl and Scarlet Spider. In the infinite Multiverse, meanwhile, there are endless Spider-Heroes! When threats arise across multiple realities, these Web-Warriors find ways to team up, combining their different strengths and skills. They are always fascinated to meet each other and—while it can get a little confusing—Peter Parker likes nothing more than calling each new counterpart a friend.

## ⊽ SPIDER-GIRL

Anya Corazon gains spider-powers after she saves a man named Miguel who turns out to be a sorcerer from a secret group, the Spider Society! When the lives of all spider-powered beings in The Multiverse are threatened, Corazon teams up with Peter Parker to help. Spider-Girl chases evil scientist Doctor Octopus in this set, joined by Spidey on his Spider-Cycle.

This Spider-Girl minifigure appears only in this set

Large web elements included in the set

**Scarlet Spider,** also known as Ben Reilly, is a clone of Spider-Man who often fights alongside him. His hoodie-wearing minifigure is not a clone, however, though it has the same head piece!

## BRICK FACTS

The Web Warriors: Ultimate Bridge Battle (set 76057) sees Spider-Girl trap Green Goblin in her web. This minifigure's appearance is based on the character Spider-Woman from Marvel's Ultimate Comics.

| Set name | Spider-Man Vs. Doc Ock | |
|---|---|---|
| **Number** 76148 | **Pieces** 234 | |
| **Year** 2020 | **Minifigures** 3 | |

## BRIDGE CHASE

Scarlet Spider was created by a villain but chooses to fight for justice. He teams up with Spider-Man to battle Scorpion and other villains in Web Warriors: Ultimate Bridge Battle (set 76057).

## GHOST-SPIDER

White hood fits over head piece

In an alternate universe, high-school student Gwen Stacy is bitten by a radioactive spider. She becomes a Super Hero with web-slinging abilities, which she often calls on to rescue her good friend Peter Parker. Known as Ghost-Spider, Stacy dons a pale, ghostly spider-suit and rides on a hover board. She chases a scary Venom Mech in this set, on a mission to rescue Peter's Aunt May.

Sticker with spider details in Ghost-Spider's colors

| Set name Spider Mech Vs. Venom | |
|---|---|
| Number 76115 | Pieces 604 |
| Year 2018 | Minifigures 4 |

Rotating stud shooters

## SPIDER-HAM

One of the strangest Spideys Peter Parker ever meets is Spider-Ham, a talking pig with a dark sense of humor. Real name Peter Porker, Spider-Ham used to be a spider—until he was bitten by a radioactive pig named May. Now a pig with spider-powers, Ham joins other Spideys to fight evil. He especially enjoys the mission in this set because he gets to eat a hot dog while riding on Spider-Man's awesome Mega-Buggy.

**Spider-Man 2099** comes from the future. Behind the mask, he is the brilliant Irish Mexican geneticist Miguel O'Hara.

**Spider-Man Noir** is from a world where everything is in black and white—including his Super Hero outfit!

Platform can launch Ham into battle

| Set name Venomosaurus Ambush | |
|---|---|
| Number 76151 | Pieces 640 |
| Year 2020 | Minifigures 4 |

**Spider-Ham's minifigure** is dressed snout-to-toe in his spider-suit. He has short legs and a unique head piece with a snout and squared ears.

LEGO® Technic pieces provide excellent suspension

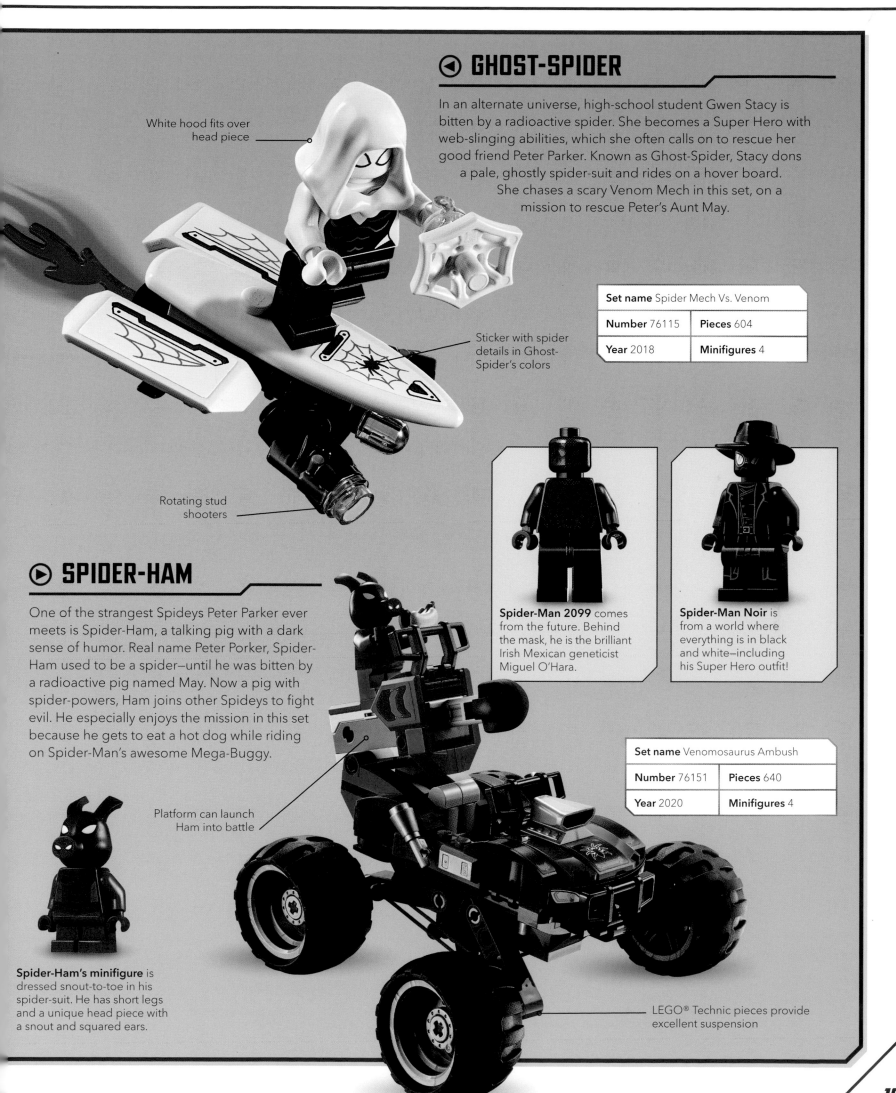

# SPIDER TECH

As a science, technology, and engineering expert, Peter Parker simply can't stop inventing and customizing vehicles for his many adventures. Some of these radical rides wouldn't look out of place at a monster truck rally or an awesome air show, while others are like nothing seen anywhere else in The Multiverse! What links them all is Spidey's iconic red-and-blue color scheme—a signal to every villain that Spider-Man and his allies are on the way...

## ⊙ SPIDER-CYCLE

The Spider-Cycle really lives up to its name, with eight spidery limbs and two sturdy wheels! The long, powerful legs make it the ideal vehicle for fighting multiarmed menace Doctor Octopus, and the whole thing can split into two for Super Hero team-ups. A row of headlight "eyes" on the front and an "abdomen" over the rear wheel complete the spidery look.

## ⊙ SPIDER-TRUCK

Sometimes Spidey wears a stealth suit, but other times he likes to be seen! This massive monster truck has many unmissable features, including balloon tires, webbed wheel rims, floodlights, Spider-Man graphics on three sides, and a huge net launcher on the roof. Villains beware!

Licence plate reads "SP1D3R #1"

Articulated legs can pivot in any direction

| Set name Spider-Man Vs. Doc Ock | |
|---|---|
| **Number** 76148 | **Pieces** 234 |
| **Year** 2020 | **Minifigures** 3 |

## SPIDER SPLIT

When Spider-Girl teams up with Spider-Man, she pilots the breakaway walking section of the Spider-Cycle while Spidey steers the motorcycle.

These front legs are on the side of the combined vehicle

Missile launchers flank front wheel

| Set name Spider-Man's Monster Truck Vs. Mysterio | |
|---|---|
| **Number** 76174 | **Pieces** 439 |
| **Year** 2021 | **Minifigures** 4 |

## ▶ SPIDER-BUGGY

This beach-style buggy has big, sturdy wheels and super suspension for springing into action on tough terrain. The rear-mounted cannon launches giant missiles clean over Spider-Man's head and includes a lookout platform for a passenger. The vehicle gives Spidey that extra bounce when he goes into battle against Venom and his prehistoric Venomosaurus beast!

| Set name | Venomosaurus Ambush | |
|---|---|---|
| Number | 76151 | Pieces 640 |
| Year | 2020 | Minifigures 4 |

Wheel position can be adjusted for a lower profile

## ◀ SPIDER-MECH

When villains such as Venom grow to giant size, Spidey uses this mighty mech to look them right in the eye! One of the Mech's arms can launch webs and robot spiders, while the other ends in a huge gripping claw. Spidey operates the mech from a cockpit in the torso, held in position by super-strong webbing straps.

Launchable robot spiders stored on arm

| Set name | Spider Mech Vs. Venom | |
|---|---|---|
| Number | 76115 | Pieces 604 |
| Year | 2018 | Minifigures 4 |

Spinning rotors provide a speedy liftoff

## ▼ SPIDERJET

Spider-Man's speediest form of transportation is this supersonic jet. It streaks across the sky as a blur of blue and red—with an added hint of black when Multiverse hero Spider-Man Noir is at the controls! The aircraft is equipped with two kinds of flick-fire missiles—perfect for chasing down Venom in his mech, or any other villains!

Spidey Noir wears 1930s-style flying goggles

Power Man steers from the forward cockpit

| Set name | Spider-Helicopter Rescue | |
|---|---|---|
| Number | 76016 | Pieces 299 |
| Year | 2014 | Characters 4 |

## ▲ SPIDER-HELICOPTER

There's room for two in this compact copter, and Spidey is happy to share it with super-pal Power Man. Together, they take on the Green Goblin as he glides through the skies above New York. If the chopper's web-shooter doesn't ground the Goblin, then its missile launchers surely will!

| Set name | Spiderjet Vs. Venom Mech | |
|---|---|---|
| Number | 76150 | Pieces 371 |
| Year | 2020 | Minifigures 3 |

# THE SPIDER LAIR

Spider-Man's brilliant base of operations is a cross between a high-tech lab, a supercomputer control center, and a teen's dream bedroom! At one end, Peter keeps his various spider-suits next to an awesome skateboard ramp. At the other, a high-security prison cell shares space with a Spidey-themed basketball hoop. In the center, a comfy swivel chair surveys six huge computer screens, ideal for both cutting-edge crime fighting and gaming—and sometimes even both at the same time!

Diagnostic report on Iron Spider armor

Detachable arms for Iron Spider armor

Camera for Peter's work at *The Daily Bugle* newspaper

Suit storage area inspired by Iron Man's armory

Parking podium for Spider-Bike

Skateboard for unwinding after tough missions

| Set name Attack on the Spider Lair | |
|---|---|
| **Number** 76175 | **Pieces** 466 |
| **Year** 2021 | **Minifigures** 6 |
| **Dimensions** 5in (14cm) high and 16in (4cm) wide | |
| **Minifigures** Spider-Man, Peter Parker, Iron Spider-Man, Ultimate Spider-Man, Green Goblin, Venom | |

**The green parts** on Spidey's stealth suit can only be seen using special lenses. Without them, it is virtually invisible.

**Peter Parker** made this simple spider-suit by customizing his everyday clothes when he first got his powers. He still likes it!

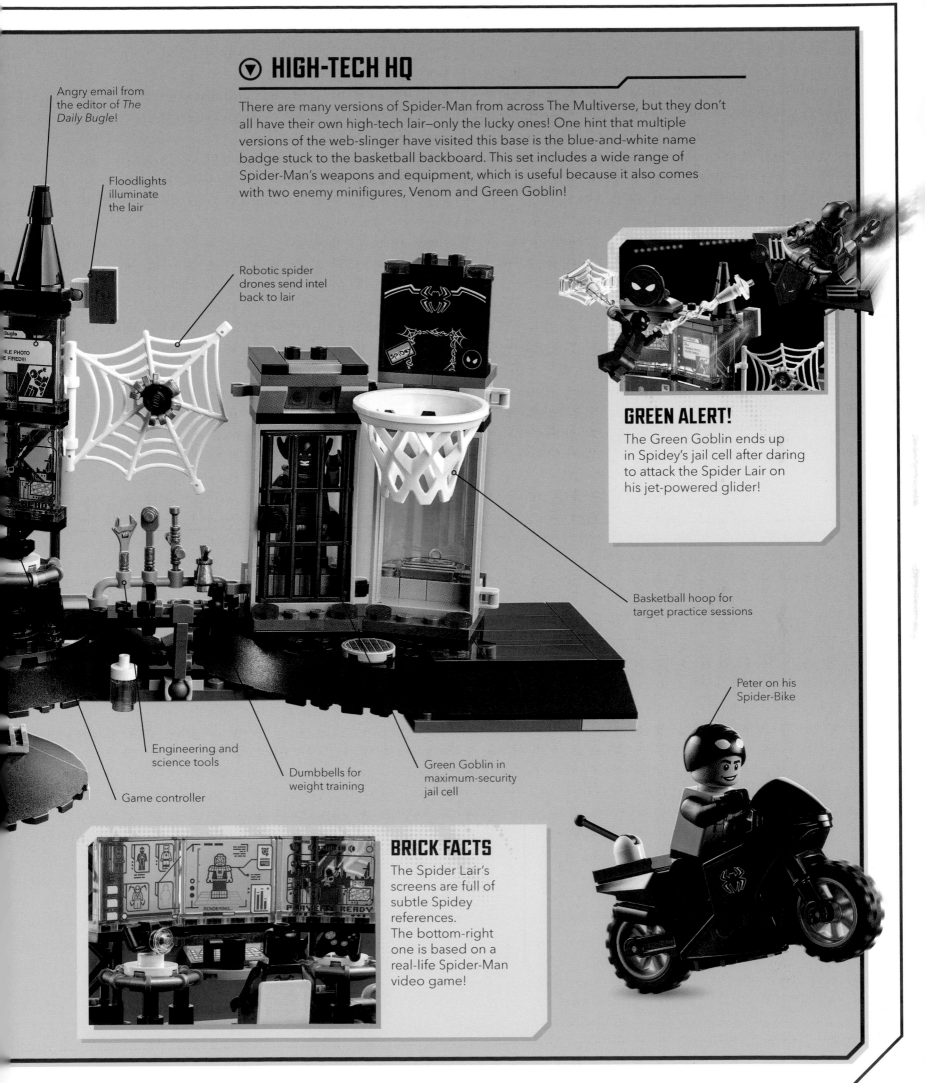

## ⊙ HIGH-TECH HQ

There are many versions of Spider-Man from across The Multiverse, but they don't all have their own high-tech lair—only the lucky ones! One hint that multiple versions of the web-slinger have visited this base is the blue-and-white name badge stuck to the basketball backboard. This set includes a wide range of Spider-Man's weapons and equipment, which is useful because it also comes with two enemy minifigures, Venom and Green Goblin!

Angry email from the editor of *The Daily Bugle*!

Floodlights illuminate the lair

Robotic spider drones send intel back to lair

### GREEN ALERT!

The Green Goblin ends up in Spidey's jail cell after daring to attack the Spider Lair on his jet-powered glider!

Basketball hoop for target practice sessions

Peter on his Spider-Bike

Engineering and science tools

Game controller

Dumbbells for weight training

Green Goblin in maximum-security jail cell

### BRICK FACTS

The Spider Lair's screens are full of subtle Spidey references. The bottom-right one is based on a real-life Spider-Man video game!

# THE DAILY BUGLE

There are many advantages to being Spider-Man, but a regular paycheck isn't one of them! So to make the money he needs to support himself and his Aunt May, Peter Parker sells photographs of Spidey in action to *The Daily Bugle* newspaper. Boss J. Jonah Jameson always prints the photos with articles that tell all sorts of lies about the "masked menace" he so despises, but at least he doesn't ask difficult questions about how Peter got his pictures!

## ◉ GOOD NEWS AND BAD

*The Daily Bugle* building is an iconic sight in Spidey's New York City. Its name stands out from the rooftop in huge red letters, while a big screen blasts its TV channel into the streets below. Some of the stories produced in the building are vital public interest ones, but others are fabricated! This four-story build is the largest LEGO® Marvel set so far, and it towers skyscraper-high over its 25 minifigures.

Mutant hero Firestar

Comms tower sends and receives the latest news

Spidey goes after Green Goblin

Signage includes an actual bugle in between the words

Doctor Octopus scales the building with ease!

Spidey's vertical-driving Spider-Mobile

Green Goblin smashes his way out of the building on his glider

## ◉ BUGLE TEAM

**J. Jonah Jameson**
The *Bugle*'s ever-angry publisher would be even more furious if he found out that his star photographer was also Spider-Man!

Ghost-Spider targets Mysterio

**Robbie Robertson**
The *Bugle*'s Editor in Chief is a cheerleader for Spider-Man who does his best to temper J. Jonah Jameson's anti-Spidey agenda.

### PENTHOUSE OFFICE

J. Jonah Jameson's top-floor office is accessed by an anteroom, where journalists wait to be grilled by their boss! Jameson's office features a computer, stacks of newspapers, and some publishing awards.

**Betty Brant**
Betty dares to stand up to Jameson while working as his secretary, earning Peter's respect. She later becomes a *Bugle* reporter.

Screen shows a villains' press conference

**Ben Urich**
This top reporter has exposed several businessmen as Super Villains, but he never reveals that he knows Peter's secret identity.

Fire escape

**Amber Grant**
Like Peter, Amber works as a freelance photographer, selling her best pictures to the *Bugle* and other New York newspapers.

A typical *Daily Bugle* front page attacking Spider-Man

**Ron Barney**
Ron is one of several *Bugle* writers who specialize in Super Hero stories. He mixes very few facts with plenty of mystery!

## NEWSROOM

The busy second-floor newsroom is where reporters write up their outlandish stories, fueled by coffee, donuts, and rolling TV news!

Big screen shows J. Jonah Jameson hosting a talk show

Peter's Aunt May runs away from Sandman

Main entrance

## PETER'S OFFICE

When Peter is in the building, he uses this freelancers' office. It's bare and dingy, with just one element of decoration: a framed Spidey photo on the back wall!

Iconic New York taxi cab

Sandman smashes through the sidewalk from underground

| Set name Daily Bugle | |
|---|---|
| **Number** 76178 | **Pieces** 3,772 |
| **Year** 2021 | **Minifigures** 25 |
| **Dimensions** 33in (82cm) tall and 11in (27cm) wide | |
| **Minifigures** 25–Amber Grant, Aunt May, Blade, Ben Urich, Bernie the Cab Driver, Betty Brant, Black Cat, Carnage, Daredevil, Doctor Octopus, Firestar, Ghost-Spider, Green Goblin, Gwen Stacy, J. Jonah Jameson, Mysterio, Peter Parker, Punisher, Robbie Robertson, Ron Barney, Sandman, Spider-Ham, Spider-Man, Venom. | |

# GREEN GOBLIN

Celebrated scientist and businessman Norman Osborn has a secret identity. As the Green Goblin, he is among the most terrifying and relentless of all Spider-Man's enemies. After discovering a chemical formula that gave him superhuman strength and cunning, Osborn created the Goblin alter ego as a simple disguise for his criminal activities. However, repeated use of the chemical has utterly confused him, to the point that he no longer knows where Norman Osborn ends and the gruesome Goblin begins!

## ▼ MONSTER MECH BATTLE

When the Goblin gets a mech with monstrous, magical powers, Spider-Man suits up with something similar. It takes their long-standing rivalry to new heights, and adds an extra level of peril for Spidey. His own mech starts to exert a dangerous mystical energy, which might turn him as wild as the Goblin!

Spider-like legs enhance the mech's muscular limbs

The living mech can see out of an eye in its chest

**The Green Goblin's** usual look is a costume, just like Spider-Man's. It includes a creepy green Halloween mask and a purple tunic.

| Set name | Spider-Man & Green Goblin Mech Battle | |
|---|---|---|
| Number | 76219 | Pieces 296 |
| Year | 2022 | Minifigures 2 |

# MEANER AND GREENER

This version of the Green Goblin isn't wearing a mask! He's been fully transformed into a hulking troll by Doctor Octopus, using a potent mix of mutant and alien DNA. He still has Norman Osborn's smarts, however, and likes to get around using the Goblin's traditional mode of transportation—a heavily armored, rocket-powered Goblin Glider.

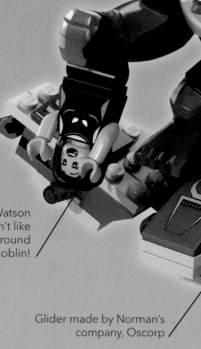

Lightweight armored suit

| Set name | Spider-Helicopter Rescue | |
| --- | --- | --- |
| **Number** 76016 | **Pieces** 299 | |
| **Year** 2014 | **Characters** 4 | |

Mary Jane Watson doesn't like hanging around with the Goblin!

Glider made by Norman's company, Oscorp

# GOBLIN GEAR

As well as his high-tech glider, the scientifically gifted Goblin uses a range of self-made weapons in his war against Spider-Man. The "bag of tricks" he carries across his shoulder contains everything from gas-filled pumpkin bombs that mess with Peter's spider-sense, to ghost bombs that trap their targets inside all-but-unbreakable bubbles!

Spidey swings in to deflect the bomb

Pumpkin bombs may be filled with gas or explosives

Goblin is rarely without his "bag of tricks"

| Set name | Spider-Man: Web Warriors Ultimate Bridge Battle | |
| --- | --- | --- |
| **Number** 76057 | **Pieces** 1,092 | |
| **Year** 2016 | **Minifigures** 7 | |

Orange outfit matches Hobgoblin's pumpkin bombs

# HOBGOBLIN GLIDER

The Green Goblin's exploits are so infamous they have even inspired copycats! The Hobgoblin flies a glider and uses pumpkin bombs just like Norman Osborn, but might be even more dangerous thanks to the upgrades he's made to Osborn's original Goblin formula. Beneath the grinning mask, he is the devious fashion designer Roderick Kingsley.

Glider shape inspired by bats' wings

| Set name | Spider-Man: Ghost Rider Team-Up | |
| --- | --- | --- |
| **Number** 76058 | **Pieces** 217 | |
| **Year** 2016 | **Minifigures** 3 | |

# DOCTOR OCTOPUS

A brilliant nuclear physicist, Otto Octavius becomes Doctor Octopus after a radiation leak accident. Octavius had created a set of mechanical tentacles to help with his work, but the accident causes them to permanently attach to his body! Turning to a life of crime as Doctor Octopus, he uses the tentacles—which he can manipulate with his mind—to help him gain money and power. Doc Ock's LEGO tentacles have been built in a variety of different ways, using all sorts of LEGO pieces across various sets.

## ▽ MECH BATTLE

Spider-Man and Doctor Octopus have been battling each other since some of Spidey's earliest comic-book adventures. Their giant armored mech suits are built using bricks in the characters' signature colors, and feature their classic weapons: Spider-Man's web-shooters and Doc Ock's mechanical tentacles. Each mech can hold a minifigure inside the cockpit so the archenemies can continue their fight in LEGO mech form.

Tentacles open and close

Web-shooter

Ball joints for posability

### BRICK FACTS

Doc Ock's mech in Spider-Man: Doc Ock's Tentacle Trap (set 76059) is a giant Octo-Bot with four detachable tentacles and six rapid shooters.

| Set name | Spider-Man & Doctor Octopus Mech Battle | |
|---|---|---|
| **Number** 76198 | | **Pieces** 305 |
| **Year** 2021 | | **Minifigures** 2 |

## ▶ SINISTER ENEMIES

Doc Ock knows that Spider-Man and other heroes such as Gwen Stacy will be tough to beat, so he enlists the help of a group of Super Villains—Mysterio, Vulture, Sandman, Electro, and Kraven the Hunter. Together, these villains are known as the Sinister Six. In this set, Spider-Man's minifigure finds himself up against Doc Ock, with large, buildable tentacles, as well as Mysterio. Spider-Gwen joins Spider-Man for the showdown.

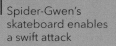

Spider-Gwen's skateboard enables a swift attack

Bag of stolen items

Tentacle built from posable connector pegs

| Set name | Spider-Man's Monster Truck Vs. Mysterio | |
|---|---|---|
| Number 76174 | Pieces 439 | |
| Year 2021 | Minifigures 4 | |

Tentacles can grab objects

## ▶ ARMORED TRUCK ATTACK

Doctor Octopus needs a constant flow of cash to keep his villainous plans in motion. So Spider-Man keeps an eye out for his foe's next robbery attempt—this time against an armored truck. Doc Ock's tentacles are incredibly powerful. A single one can support his weight while the others lift heavy objects or tear apart metal containers.

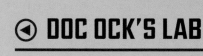

| Set name | Doc Ock Truck Heist | |
|---|---|---|
| Number 76015 | Pieces 237 | |
| Year 2014 | Minifigures 3 | |

Back of truck blows open

Air vent shaft

Power cables

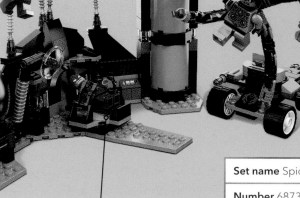

## ◀ DOC OCK'S LAB

Doc Ock's intelligence is one reason he remains one of Spider-Man's most challenging opponents. The villain's lab is outfitted with a containment cell, an examination table, and all sorts of high-tech equipment. In this set, Spidey breaches the lab to rescue one of his allies, Iron Fist—who Doc Ock has kidnapped in an attempt to steal his powers.

Examination table

| Set name | Spider-Man's Doc Ock Ambush | |
|---|---|---|
| Number 6873 | Pieces 295 | |
| Year 2012 | Minifigures 3 | |

**Martial arts master**
Iron Fist is a friend to Spider-Man. His minifigure is exclusive to this set.

# VENOM

Venom is an alien symbiote, a creature from a faraway planet that can think for itself but needs to bond with another living being (known as a host) so it can take form. It arrives on Earth as a black, gooey, fast-moving liquid, searching for a new host. When Venom bonds with a host, it bonds with their mind as well as their body. Some parts of the host's personality will change, especially when it comes to aggression. Bonded with a host, Venom is incredibly strong, can heal fast, and can shape-shift into much larger forms.

**When Venom first bonds** with Spider-Man, it takes the form of a black-and-white Spidey-Suit. At first, Spidey enjoys the power boost, but he rejects the suit when he realizes he's not quite himself.

## ⏵ VENOMOSAURUS

In Marvel comic-book adventures, Venom bonds with a variety of hosts—including a dinosaur! Venom protects the dinosaur's LEGO egg from intruders, who include Spider-Man, Iron Spider, and Spider-Ham. The Spider-Ham minifigure (also known as Peter Porker, a talking pig version of Spider-Man), first appeared in this set.

| Set name Venomosaurus Ambush | |
|---|---|
| Number 76151 | Pieces 640 |
| Year 2020 | Minifigures 4 |

### BRICK FACTS

A compartment opens up at the back of the Venomosaurus revealing enough space to fit one very unlucky minifigure.

Jaws can shut if tongue piece is removed

Venom minifigure clips onto the back of the Venomosaurus

Venom egg

# MECH AND MAY

Venom and Spider-Man are frequent foes, and come up against each other often. In this set, a powerful Venom mech takes off with Peter Parker's Aunt May in his mighty grasp. A Venom minifigure controls the mech, which towers tall over regular minifigures. The mech has many of Venom's classic features, including wavy tentacles, sharp teeth, and a super-long tongue.

| Set name | Spider Mech Vs. Venom | |
|---|---|---|
| **Number** 76115 | **Pieces** 604 | |
| **Year** 2018 | **Minifigures** 4 | |

Terrifying tongue made from two LEGO pieces

| Set name | Spider-Man Vs. The Venom Symbiote | |
|---|---|---|
| **Number** 30448 | **Pieces** 49 | |
| **Year** 2016 | **Minifigures** 1 | |

All five heads are identical

Four lower legs support the build

## SPIDER ATTACK

Venom takes on many terrifying forms with different hosts. Perhaps the scariest is the Venom from this polybag set, where it walks on poky, spidery legs and has five grinning heads. A Spider-Man minifigure joins the battle with a LEGO super-jumper piece to help him knock Venom off balance, and hopefully slow down the monster.

## IRON VENOM

Venom bonds with Iron Man to create Iron Venom. The resulting Venom Crawler has eight scuttling legs and a scorpion-like rear stud shooter. The set also comes with Spider-Man, Iron Venom, and another villainous minifigure, Carnage, which means Spidey will need to call on all his powers to win this battle!

| Set name | Venom Crawler | |
|---|---|---|
| **Number** 76163 | **Pieces** 413 | |
| **Year** 2020 | **Minifigures** 3 | |

Eight posable legs

Iron Venom controls the Venom Crawler

**Pork Grind** is a Venom/Spider-Ham villain on Earth-8311, a dimension filled with talking animals.

**The second** minifigure version of Iron Venom comes in set 40454. Its helmet and armor is half Venom, half Iron Man.

### BRICK FACTS

Another Venom mech comes in set 76150, where it faces off against Spidey, Spider-Man Noir, and the Spiderjet.

# VULTURE

In the world of Marvel Comics, Adrian Toomes, also known as Vulture, uses his flight harness to take to the air so he can commit crimes. Vulture is a member of the Sinister Six along with Doctor Octopus, Electro, Sandman, Kraven the Hunter, and Mysterio. He and the rest of the Sinister Six regularly find themselves facing off against Spider-Man, who is on a mission to stop them from committing their evil crimes.

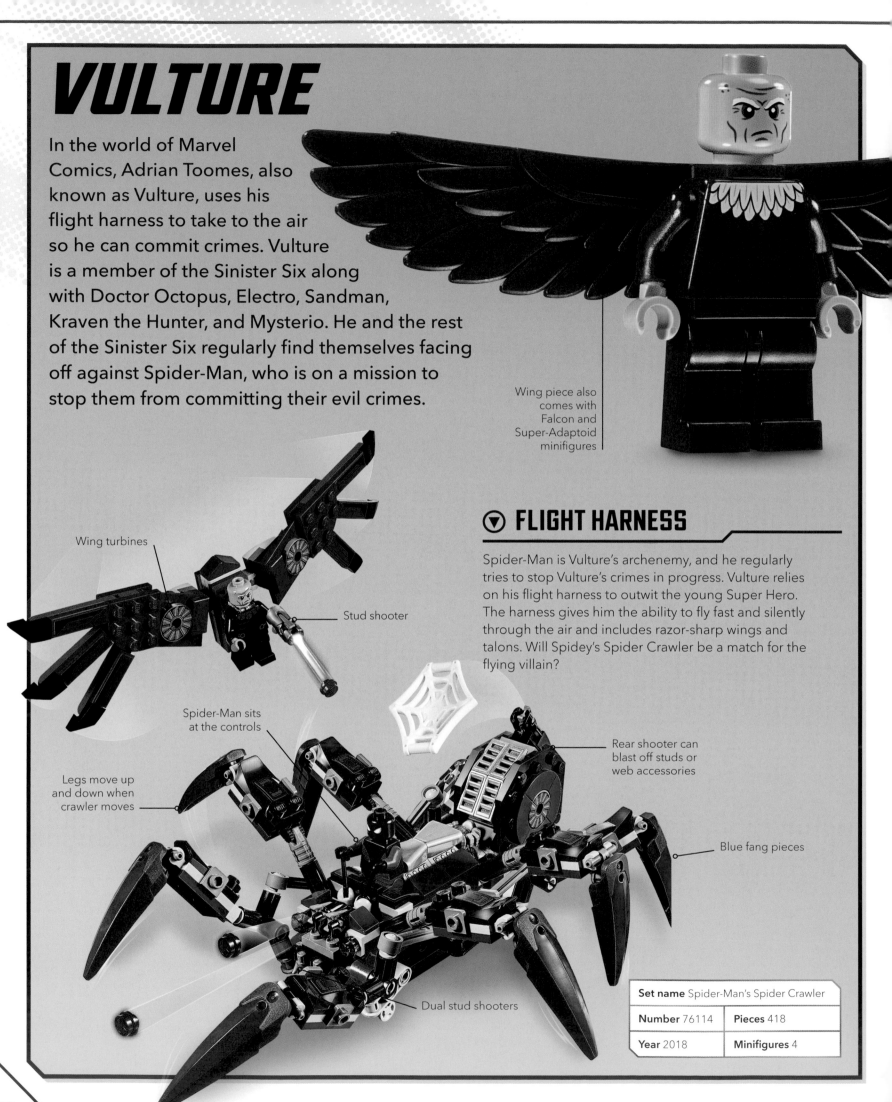

Wing piece also comes with Falcon and Super-Adaptoid minifigures

Wing turbines

Stud shooter

## ⊙ FLIGHT HARNESS

Spider-Man is Vulture's archenemy, and he regularly tries to stop Vulture's crimes in progress. Vulture relies on his flight harness to outwit the young Super Hero. The harness gives him the ability to fly fast and silently through the air and includes razor-sharp wings and talons. Will Spidey's Spider Crawler be a match for the flying villain?

Spider-Man sits at the controls

Legs move up and down when crawler moves

Rear shooter can blast off studs or web accessories

Blue fang pieces

Dual stud shooters

| Set name | Spider-Man's Spider Crawler | |
|---|---|---|
| Number 76114 | | Pieces 418 |
| Year 2018 | | Minifigures 4 |

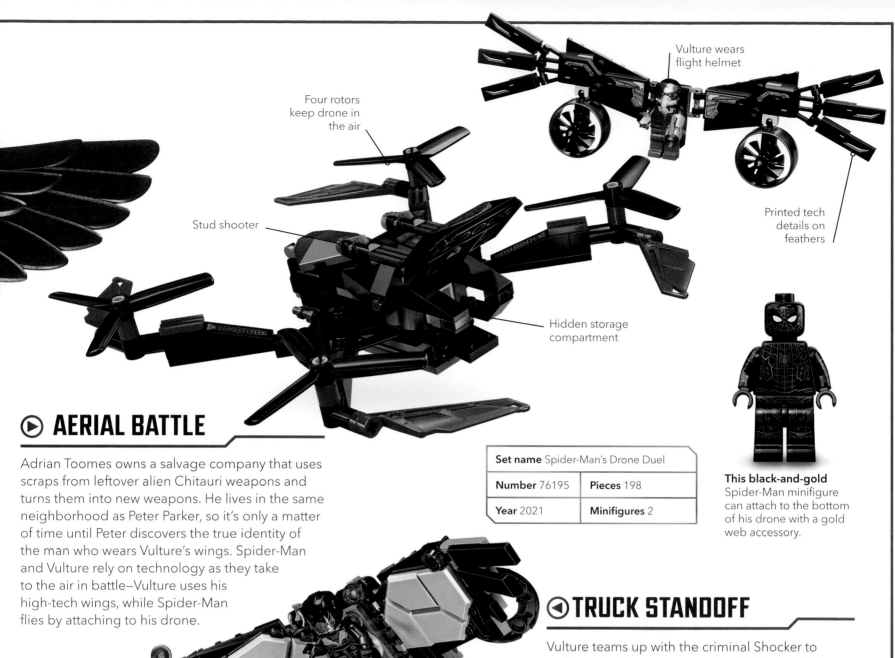

Four rotors keep drone in the air

Vulture wears flight helmet

Printed tech details on feathers

Stud shooter

Hidden storage compartment

## ▶ AERIAL BATTLE

Adrian Toomes owns a salvage company that uses scraps from leftover alien Chitauri weapons and turns them into new weapons. He lives in the same neighborhood as Peter Parker, so it's only a matter of time until Peter discovers the true identity of the man who wears Vulture's wings. Spider-Man and Vulture rely on technology as they take to the air in battle—Vulture uses his high-tech wings, while Spider-Man flies by attaching to his drone.

| Set name Spider-Man's Drone Duel | |
|---|---|
| **Number** 76195 | **Pieces** 198 |
| **Year** 2021 | **Minifigures** 2 |

**This black-and-gold** Spider-Man minifigure can attach to the bottom of his drone with a gold web accessory.

Huge flight harness includes detachable stud shooters

## ◀ TRUCK STANDOFF

Vulture teams up with the criminal Shocker to make and sell weapons on the criminal market. When Spider-Man and Iron Man try to stop them, the villains' high-tech accessories prove more than a match. Vulture's formidable flight harness helps him stay above the action, while Shocker's van conceals much more than boxes of illegal goods—a rapid-shooter powered by alien technology rises up from the back!

Spider-Man sticks to truck with extra-long web

Iron Man boosters

Shocker's van conceals weapon in the back

| Set name Beware the Vulture | |
|---|---|
| **Number** 76083 | **Pieces** 375 |
| **Year** 2017 | **Minifigures** 4 |

**Shocker is a salvage worker** turned criminal who works for the Vulture. His minifigure comes with two power fists.

# MYSTERIO

Quentin Beck is a special effects artist and former employee at Stark Industries. He never felt appreciated by Tony Stark and, after hearing of Iron Man's death, seeks to become the world's next great Super Hero. Mysterio creates illusions using drones and holograms to make people believe the planet is under threat. While Beck has no super-powers at all, his tech expertise and talent for building believable illusions convince even Spider-Man. With each new illusion, Beck swoops to the rescue as the caped "hero" Mysterio.

Helmet protects Mysterio's true identity

Green stand looks like swirling puffs of smoke

## ▼ WATER ILLUSION

When Peter Parker takes a trip to Venice, Italy, with his classmates, he's hoping for some much-needed downtime. But Mysterio has other ideas. He uses advanced projectors and drones to create the illusion that a giant water creature is wreaking havoc on Venice's Grand Canal, and Parker leaps into action, using his spider-powers to save passers-by. Meanwhile, Mysterio arrives to save the day in style.

Top of Venice tower

Peter Parker leaps into action

Based on the Rialto bridge in Venice

### BRICK FACTS

A trigger on the back of the bridge causes the center of the bridge to explode. Amid the debris are some LEGO accessories, including a rat, a slice of pizza, and a red ruby.

MJ tries to help from her gondola

Hydro-Man minifigure's base makes it look like he's rising out of the water

Press to flip the table amid the chaos

| Set name | Hydro-Man Attack | |
| --- | --- | --- |
| Number | 76129 | Pieces 471 |
| Year | 2019 | Minifigures 4 |

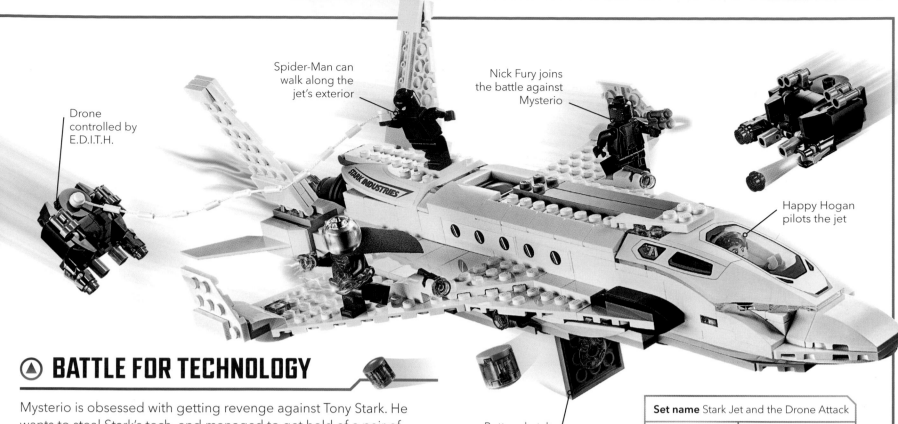

Drone controlled by E.D.I.T.H.

Spider-Man can walk along the jet's exterior

Nick Fury joins the battle against Mysterio

Happy Hogan pilots the jet

# ◬ BATTLE FOR TECHNOLOGY

Mysterio is obsessed with getting revenge against Tony Stark. He wants to steal Stark's tech, and managed to get hold of a pair of glasses that Stark left to Peter Parker. The glasses allow Mysterio to control E.D.I.T.H., Stark's advanced intelligence system. While projecting a terrifying illusion over London, England, Mysterio uses E.D.I.T.H. to destroy Stark's jet and send drones to attack Spider-Man.

Bottom hatch pops open

| Set name Stark Jet and the Drone Attack | |
|---|---|
| **Number** 76130 | **Pieces** 504 |
| **Year** 2019 | **Minifigures** 4 |

**The Spidey stealth suit** debuted in Molten Man Battle (set 76128). It has black-and-gray coloring and details showing pockets, a belt, and a zipper.

| Set name Molten Man Battle | |
|---|---|
| **Number** 76128 | **Pieces** 294 |
| **Year** 2019 | **Minifigures** 3 |

# ▶ FIRE ILLUSION

Mysterio projects the illusion of a fiery monster attacking a carnival in Prague, Czech Republic. The LEGO monster shows its true destructive power by incorporating partially melted objects into its build, such as a traffic light, a road sign, and half a car! A firefighter minifigure is included in the set as well, though it's doubtful they will be very helpful in this situation.

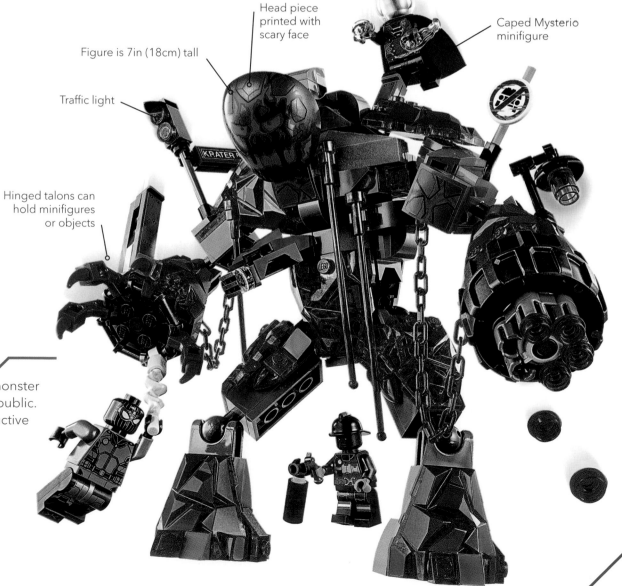

Head piece printed with scary face

Figure is 7in (18cm) tall

Caped Mysterio minifigure

Traffic light

Hinged talons can hold minifigures or objects

# SANDMAN

Escaped convict William Baker is exposed to dangerous radiation, which gives him the ability to transform his body into sand and morph into various forms. Known as the Sandman, Baker uses his super-powers to gain the upper hand in battle by changing his hands into weapons or evading blows from opponents by dissolving into grains of sand. Sandman frequently faces off against Spider-Man and is a founding member of the Super Villain gang the Sinister Six, but occasionally Sandman and Spider-Man find themselves fighting on the same side.

## ▽ TRANSFORMATION

Sandman can be difficult to beat in hand-to-hand combat because he can grow into supersized forms. His minifigure sometimes comes with a base of swirling sand instead of legs, which shows his body mid-transformation.

Sand-colored face, hair, and eyes

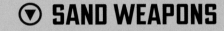

Transitions into sand

| Set name Spider-Man's Spider Crawler | |
|---|---|
| Number 76114 | Pieces 418 |
| Year 2018 | Minifigures 4 |

Sand piece makes Sandman taller than regular minifigures

## ▽ SAND WEAPONS

Sandman can change parts of his body into tightly packed sand that is hard as rock—useful for stopping enemies during a crime spree. In this set Sandman makes the most of his powers, turning one hand into a large hammer and creating a large sand hand to grab hold of Iron Spider.

## BRICK FACTS

Sandman's minifigure has an additional buildable base, to help him tower over other minifigures even more. The base conceals a secret compartment that holds Sandman's stolen gems.

| Set name Rhino and Sandman Super Villain Team-Up | |
|---|---|
| Number 76037 | Pieces 386 |
| Year 2015 | Minifigures 4 |

# CARNAGE

Like Spider-Man's frequent enemy Venom, Carnage is an alien symbiote that needs to attach to a host to take form. Carnage chooses the vicious murderer Cletus Kasady as his host. The symbiote villain sees no value in life and craves destruction and chaos. He morphs parts of his red body into dangerous weapons, making him fast, powerful, and almost impossible to stop.

Adjustable floodlights

Reinforced bumper

| Set name Spider-Man: Venom Crawler | |
|---|---|
| Number 76163 | Pieces 413 |
| Year 2020 | Minifigures 3 |

## ◉ VERSUS SPIDER-MAN

With Kasady as his host Carnage is incredibly strong, so Spider-Man leaps into his Spider-Buggy and sets off to stop the villain's rampage. In this set, Carnage's minifigure has no tentacle attachments, but he does wield a deadly mace—which Spidey hopes won't damage the buggy's red-and-blue paint job.

## ▶ GHOST RIDER TEAM-UP

Carnage's minifigure has a cool configuration of tentacles in this set, with four identical tentacles attached to a bracket that goes around his neck. This time, he is pursued by Spider-Man and Ghost Rider in Ghost Rider's flame-covered black car. The car is equipped with stud shooters, but will that be enough to stop Carnage?

Car seats one

Flames for hair

Tentacles trail behind Carnage as he flees

**There are two** Ghost Rider minifigures. One is based on the character Johnny Blaze (set 76058), while this one is based on car mechanic Robbie Reyes.

| Set name Spider-Man and Ghost Rider Vs. Carnage | |
|---|---|
| Number 76173 | Pieces 212 |
| Year 2021 | Minifigures 3 |

# ASSORTED ENEMIES

Spider-Man has his hands full both at home—in his local New York City borough, Queens—and around the world, fighting mercenaries and taking down criminals. Some villains seek fame and fortune, others desire world domination, and some want nothing more than to personally defeat Spider-Man. Spidey is ready and willing to face his foes one-on-one or as a group, such as when they've teamed up with other Super Villains in organizations including the Sinister Six or the Frightful Four.

## ▽ DOCTOR DOOM'S JET

Victor von Doom assumes the name Doctor Doom after he takes over the small European country Latveria. While Doctor Doom is one of the Fantastic Four's greatest enemies, his desire to rule the world also puts him at odds with Spider-Man. Doom's Doomjet includes two stud missiles, which it uses to attack Spider-Man's place of work, the *Daily Bugle* office.

Latverian flag sticker

Cockpit fits one minifigure

## ▽ SPIDER-TRIKE BATTLE

Electro, who has the power to control electricity, is a frequent Spider-Man foe. He menaces New York City by forming and wielding weapons out of electricity. Spider-Man takes to his Spider-Trike to defeat Electro, using its launch ability to gain the upper hand. But Spidey will have to be quick to capture Electro, who can slide down power lines and absorb electricity from nearby objects.

Ejector seat

Electricity bolts

| Set name Spider-Man: Daily Bugle Showdown | |
|---|---|
| Number 76005 | Pieces 476 |
| Year 2013 | Minifigures 5 |

| Set name Spider-Trike Vs. Electro | |
|---|---|
| Number 76014 | Pieces 70 |
| Year 2014 | Minifigures 2 |

**Only one Doctor Doom** minifigure has been released to date, and he wears a green cape and hood to shroud his sinister face.

**Beetle works with** various villains, including Doctor Doom. His minifigure wears his homemade mechanical suit, which gives him superhuman strength.

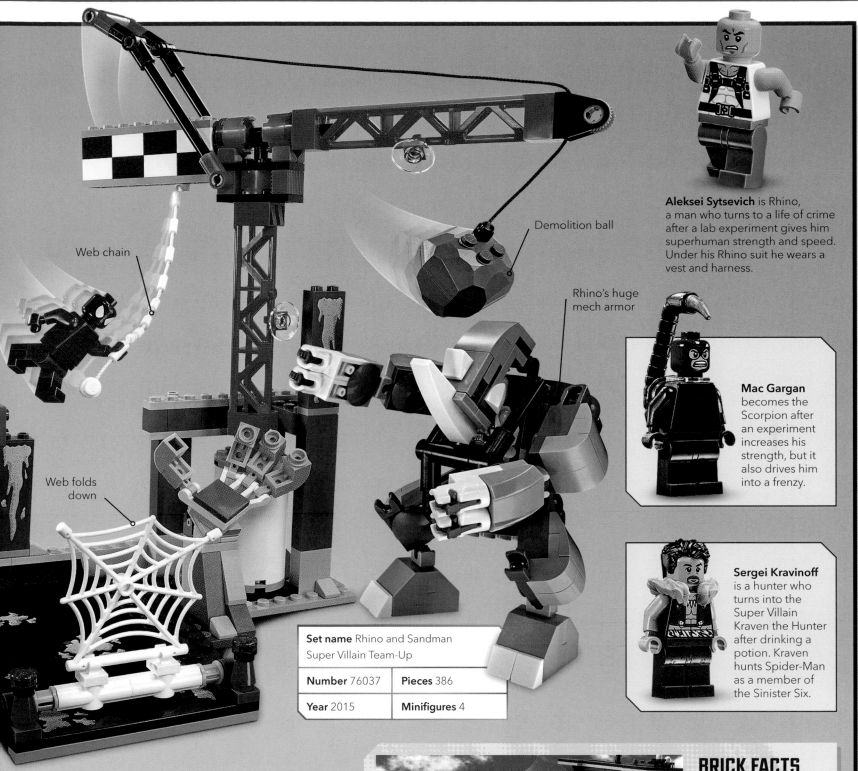

Web chain

Demolition ball

**Aleksei Sytsevich** is Rhino, a man who turns to a life of crime after a lab experiment gives him superhuman strength and speed. Under his Rhino suit he wears a vest and harness.

Rhino's huge mech armor

Web folds down

**Mac Gargan** becomes the Scorpion after an experiment increases his strength, but it also drives him into a frenzy.

**Sergei Kravinoff** is a hunter who turns into the Super Villain Kraven the Hunter after drinking a potion. Kraven hunts Spider-Man as a member of the Sinister Six.

| **Set name** Rhino and Sandman Super Villain Team-Up | |
|---|---|
| **Number** 76037 | **Pieces** 386 |
| **Year** 2015 | **Minifigures** 4 |

## 🔺 RHINO & SANDMAN

Villains Sandman and Rhino team up to steal precious diamonds, but they are quickly tracked down by Spider-Man and Iron Spider. A showdown takes place at a construction site, where a tall, rotating crane provides many perilous battle opportunities.

### BRICK FACTS

Spider-Man faces villains aplenty in the 1,092-piece Web Warriors: Ultimate Bridge Battle (set 76057). The set comes with seven minifigures including Spider-Man, Aunt May, Spider-Girl, and Scarlet Spider, and foes Green Goblin, Scorpion, and Kraven the Hunter.

# ASSORTED ALLIES

Spider-Man has a lot of enemies, but he also has a long list of friends and allies he can turn to for help, advice, or just some company while protecting the neighborhood. Some of Spidey's allies are consistently on the side of truth and justice, while others have more complicated pasts and motivations. Some turn out to be allies against a common enemy, or just for a specific mission.

Fire chain for catching foes

Flaming hair part of head piece

Large back wheel for extra power

| Set name Spider-Man: Ghost Rider Team-Up | |
|---|---|
| Number 76058 | Pieces 217 |
| Year 2016 | Minifigures 3 |

## ▶ GHOST RIDER

Spider-Man and Ghost Rider don't have much in common—apart from a few enemies, such as the demon Mephisto. The first Ghost Rider, Johnny Blaze, gives his soul to Mephisto to save his father's life. But making a deal with a demon never ends well, and Blaze's body and motorcycle are consumed by hellfire as he fights against villains. Ghost Rider's Hell Cycle comes complete with LEGO hellfire pieces at the front and back.

Side armor plates

### Daredevil
Some call Daredevil a vigilante, but attorney-by-day Matt Murdock fights criminals in his spare time, wearing his trademark red suit.

### Firestar
A mutant with the power to manipulate microwave radiation, Firestar debuted in the animated series *Spider-Man and His Amazing Friends*.

### Nova
Like Peter Parker, Sam Alexander becomes a Super Hero when he is just a teenager. As Nova, Sam works with the intergalactic peacekeeping force Nova Corps.

### Blade
Part human, part vampire, Blade is on an eternal mission to destroy all vampires. He is an expert martial artist and often uses daggers to take down his opponents.

### Black Cat
Black Cat continues her father's legacy as a cat burglar, but she has been known to team up with Spider-Man to take on villains such as Doctor Octopus and Kingpin.

Fire elements show motorcycle in flames

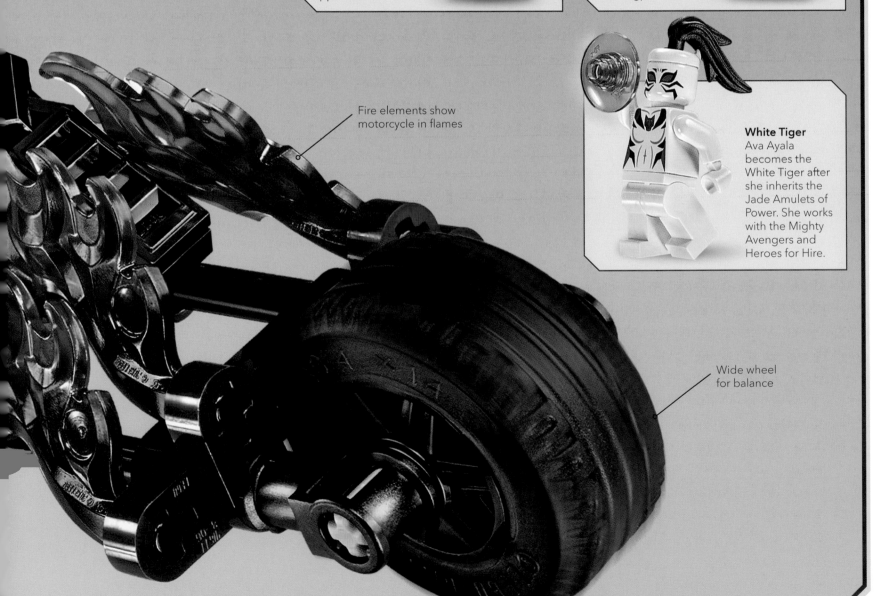

### White Tiger
Ava Ayala becomes the White Tiger after she inherits the Jade Amulets of Power. She works with the Mighty Avengers and Heroes for Hire.

Wide wheel for balance

# IRON MAN

A bold and brilliant inventor, Tony Stark created the first Iron Man armor to escape after being kidnapped. As one of the founding members of the Avengers and the CEO of Stark Industries, Stark has access to all the money and materials he needs to refine his Iron Man armor over the years, creating dozens of Iron Man suits to fight criminals around the world. Stark also mentors fellow Avenger Peter Parker on his Spider-Man journey, offering the young Super Hero technology and advice.

## ▽ MALIBU MANSION

Tony Stark and his home are in jeopardy when an intruder in a helicopter attacks. Stark's mansion is full of high-tech equipment, weapons, tools, and Iron Man suits, but will it be enough to withstand an enemy attack? This set includes the robot arm DUM-E and five minifigures, including unique versions of Tony Stark and Pepper Potts.

| Set name Iron Man: Malibu Mansion Attack | |
|---|---|
| **Number** 76007 | **Pieces** 364 |
| **Year** 2013 | **Minifigures** 5 |

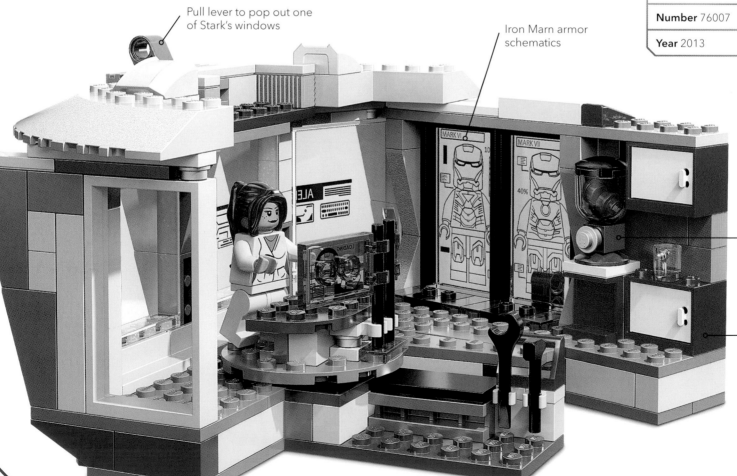

Pull lever to pop out one of Stark's windows

Iron Marn armor schematics

Kitchen area, complete with blender

Kitchen cabinet

# IRON MAN ARMOR

**Mark 1**
Iron Man's Mark 1 armor is his first Iron Man suit, created out of the limited supplies he has while being held prisoner by The Ten Rings criminal group.

**Mark 2**
Iron Man's second suit is a more refined and efficient version of the Mark 1 armor. This minifigure is exclusive to Iron Man Armory (set 76216).

**Mark 3**
Iron Man's Mark 3 armor is the first to include the iconic red-and-gold color scheme and includes an integrated weapons system in its design.

**Mark 5**
Tony Stark creates a more portable suit with his Mark 5 armor. It can fit inside a briefcase-sized container, which makes it ideal for travel.

**Mark 22**
Iron Man's Mark 22 armor has gray-and-red coloring and flame designs over the lower legs. It is exclusive to Avengers Tower Battle (set 76166).

**Mark 25**
Created for construction jobs, the Mark 25 armor is destroyed during the Clean Slate Protocol that wipes out Stark's Iron Legion after the Battle on the *Norco*.

**Mark 30**
Iron Man's blue armor variant, the Mark 30 suit, is a part of the Iron Legion. The suit contains hidden blades and joins the fight in Avengers Tower Battle (set 76166).

**Mark 41**
The Mark 41 armor is a part of Iron Man's protective Iron Legion. This minifigure is part of the Iron Man Hall of Armor (set 76125).

**Mark 50**
The Mark 50 Iron Man suit is the first to include nanotechnology. Stark uses this suit when fighting Thanos on Titan.

**Mark 85**
The Mark 85 armor is the strongest, most versatile suit Stark creates. The minifigure comes with wings that Iron Man puts to use during the Battle of Earth.

## BRICK FACTS

The minifigure behind the armors has black spiky hair and wears a black-and-gold top. Stark's head piece comes with both a smirk and a scowl, and can be found in three LEGO® sets.

## SCUBA IRON MAN

In his comic-book adventures, Iron Man dresses in full scuba gear to take on his enemies. In Iron Skull Sub Attack (set 76048), Scuba Iron Man is joined by Captain America to take on Iron Skull and Hydra under the water.

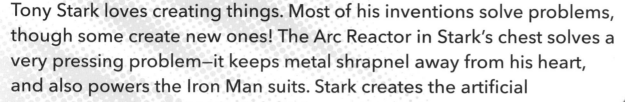

# TONY STARK'S TECH

Tony Stark loves creating things. Most of his inventions solve problems, though some create new ones! The Arc Reactor in Stark's chest solves a very pressing problem—it keeps metal shrapnel away from his heart, and also powers the Iron Man suits. Stark creates the artificial intelligence program JARVIS to help him make upgrades to dozens of different Iron Man armor versions, but another of his AI creations, Ultron, wreaks havoc around the world until it is destroyed.

Fingers can open and close into a fist

One minifigure fits inside

Legs are posable

| Set name The Hulkbuster: The Battle of Wakanda | |
|---|---|
| **Number** 76247 | **Pieces** 385 |
| **Year** 2023 | **Minifigures** 4 |

Feet are attached with ball joints

Three toes can move independently

**The artificial intelligence** program that runs the Hulkbuster armor is nicknamed Veronica.

## ⏵ HULKBUSTER

Stark first develops the Hulkbuster armor so he can stop Bruce Banner from wreaking havoc when he turns into the angry Hulk. Banner later uses an upgraded version of the armor to fight Thanos's army in Wakanda. Wearing this super-sized armor, Banner has the same strength as Hulk with the addition of weapons found in most Iron Man armor, such as repulsors.

# ▶ STARK JET

Tony Stark's inventions continue to help Peter Parker even after Stark is gone. Happy Hogan, Stark's friend and former bodyguard, brings Stark's white private jet to Europe so Peter can create a new Spider-Man suit using the tech inside. This is the only set that includes a Happy Hogan minifigure.

Button opens bottom hatch for Spider-Man or energy bombs

Adjustable wings

Two minifigures fit inside cockpit

Sleek build means jet can travel fast

| Set name Stark Jet and the Drone Attack | |
| --- | --- |
| Number 76130 | Pieces 504 |
| Year 2019 | Minifigures 4 |

## VINTAGE CAR

Stark loves to take apart and reinvent old machines. He keeps a classic roadster in the Iron Man Armory (set 76167) in his mansion to tinker with during his free time.

## BRICK FACTS

Stark always travels in style. To get to his destinations fast, he favors cool cars like this sleek, white convertible, which comes in a newer version of Iron Man Armory (set 76216).

## ◀ IGOR

When Tony Stark calls for the Iron Legion's help during the Battle on the *Norco*, the brute strength of the Iron Man Mark 38 armor (codenamed Igor) comes in handy. Igor was destroyed, like the rest of the Iron Legion, during the Clean Slate Protocol, though the LEGO version features a very sturdy build.

| Set name Iron Man Hall of Armor | |
| --- | --- |
| Number 76125 | Pieces 524 |
| Year 2019 | Minifigures 6 |

Individual fingers can articulate

A minifigure can fit inside Igor

**The robotic arm**
DUM-E helps Stark assemble the Iron Man armor.

# AVENGERS TOWER

Avengers Tower, previously known as Stark Tower, is built by Tony Stark and serves as the base for the Avengers in New York City. The imposing tower houses an armory, a tech lab, and a prison cell to hold any unwanted visitors. Unfortunately, any place where the Avengers meet up to make plans, conduct experiments, or just enjoy each other's company will always be a target for criminals, such as agents from the rogue government think tank AIM, and Red Skull, a military strategist and Captain America's archenemy.

## CHILL TIME

Iron Man and Black Widow find some time to relax, though they haven't yet realized that an AIM agent hovers outside the window behind them.

One AIM agent minifigure comes with a grappling hook to scale the tower

Observation deck

The tower is 17in (43cm) high

## TECH LAB

The lab at Avengers Tower is equipped to analyze items from Earth and beyond, including one of the two Infinity Stones that come with this set.

## PRISON CELL

Electrified bars open and shut in the front of the cell to keep prisoners in, while a button pops out the back door when it's time for a prison breakout.

Balcony can collapse

## WEAPONS RACK

Black Widow's blasters and Hawkeye's bow are just a few of the weapons stored here. Behind the rack lies the Infinity Gauntlet.

The five-story tower opens up to reveal seven rooms

## ARC REACTOR ROOM

The tower's power source is housed on the ground floor. Stickers include directions on how to power and control the reactor, which was first developed by Howard Stark.

## ARMORY

Some of Iron Man's spare suits are stored in the armory. The Mark 22 and Mark 30 armor minifigures (also known as "Blazer" and "Tazer") are exclusive to this set.

## GARAGE

The Avenger's Tower garage contains a Sky-Cycle—a flying motorcycle used by Black Widow, Captain America, and Hawkeye. It seats one minifigure.

| Set name | Avengers Tower Battle | |
| --- | --- | --- |
| Number 76166 | | Pieces 685 |
| Year 2020 | | Minifigures 7 |

# CAPTAIN AMERICA

Steve Rogers wants to fight for his country so much during World War II that he volunteers to be part of the experimental Super Soldier Program. A serum is injected into Rogers that makes him stronger and faster with incredibly quick reflexes. Dubbed "Captain America," and armed with a shield made from vibranium, Rogers fights against his country's deadliest enemies, including Hydra. When he is revived from a decades-long Arctic slumber following a plane crash, Captain America joins the Avengers and fights with them in many battles.

Taskforce stickers on both sides of truck

Front blasters can move up and down

All-terrain tires

| Set name | Black Panther Pursuit | |
|---|---|---|
| Number 76047 | Pieces 287 | |
| Year 2016 | Minifigures 3 | |

## ⏺ JEEP CHASE

Captain America finds himself facing off against Black Panther because Cap remains loyal to his old friend Bucky Barnes. Black Panther is hot on Bucky's tail because he wrongly believes that Bucky killed his father. Captain America's jeep is up to the chase, with its sturdy tires and front missile shooters.

# ▼ MOTORCYCLE ATTACK

Captain America will do whatever it takes to defeat Thanos and his armies. Cap calls for all Avengers to assemble for the Battle of Earth, where he speeds into the fray taking on hordes of Thanos's soldiers, including the Chitauri, Sakaarans, and Outriders. Cap's sturdy motorcycle features both the Avengers and Captain America insignia, and is equipped with disc shooters, detachable blasters, and scorching exhaust flames!

Exhaust flame

Shield storage

| Set name | Captain America: Outriders Attack | |
|---|---|---|
| **Number** 76123 | | **Pieces** 167 |
| **Year** 2019 | | **Minifigures** 4 |

Bike kickstand underneath

Disc shooters shoot shields at enemies

**At the Battle** of Wakanda, Cap's head piece is printed with his beard, and his minifigure holds two powerful Wakandan shields.

## HYDRA STOMPER

In another universe where Peggy Carter becomes Captain Carter, the first Avenger, Steve Rogers dons the Hydra Stomper armor to fight against Hydra.

# HYDRA

An ancient, secret criminal organization, Hydra's main objective is nothing less than world domination. Hydra agents search for powerful relics from other worlds, such as the Tesseract and the Mind Stone, which puts them at odds with the Avengers and S.H.I.E.L.D. Hydra is also responsible for brainwashing the American soldier Bucky Barnes and turning him into the Winter Soldier.

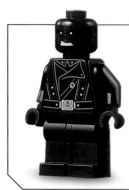

**During WWII,** Hydra's leader is Johann Schmidt who becomes the Red Skull after giving himself the Super Soldier Serum.

| Set name The Hydra Fortress Smash | |
|---|---|
| **Number** 76041 | **Pieces** 405 |
| **Year** 2015 | **Characters** 5 |

Hulk "big fig" figure

## ▶ HULK SMASH

Hulk and fellow Avengers Iron Man, Captain America, Thor, Black Widow, and Hawkeye fight off soldiers outside a secret Hydra base in Sokovia while searching for Loki's scepter. Hulk summons all of his strength and fury to smash aside any Hydra vehicles or henchmen that stand in his way.

Hit front of vehicle to pop off top weapons

**Hydra soldiers** wear light-colored uniforms to blend in with the snow on Sokovia, and goggles to help with the glare.

**Baron Strucker** is a Hydra leader who uses Loki's scepter to carry out experiments at the Hydra research base.

Top gun turret detaches

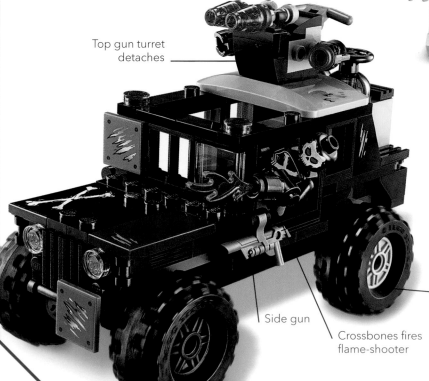

## ◀ CROSSBONES TRUCK

Brock Rumlow, codenamed Crossbones, is a Hydra agent who infiltrates S.H.I.E.L.D. without anyone realizing. But after he steals a biological weapon, Captain America, Falcon, Black Widow, and Wanda Maximoff pursue him through the streets of Lagos, Nigeria. The Crossbones truck set includes a lever that shoots the explosives stored in the back up into the air.

Rugged tires suited to bumpy roads

Side gun

Crossbones fires flame-shooter

| Set name Crossbones' Hazard Heist | |
|---|---|
| **Number** 76050 | **Pieces** 179 |
| **Year** 2016 | **Minifigures** 3 |

# AIM

Government-funded organization Advanced Idea Mechanics—also known as AIM—is tasked with supporting scientific research. Founded by research scientist Aldrich Killian, AIM can be credited with the creation of many cutting-edge programs and high-tech breakthroughs. However, the pursuit of scientific advancement regularly leads to sinister actions, and Killian ends up trying to take control of the United States.

**AIM founder**
Aldrich Killian creates the Extremis serum along with Dr. Maya Hansen. It gives humans the ability to heal and regenerate.

## ▶ AIM JET PACK

In the comics, AIM is heavily aligned with Hydra and its goals of world domination. LEGO AIM agents appear in several sets, where they are usually up to no good. In this set, a daring AIM agent uses his jet pack to make a quick getaway with a haul of biochemical weapons. The agent's jet pack is stocked with an assortment of weapons, including stud shooters, saw blades, and a grappling hook shooter.

| Set name Avengers Speeder Bike Attack | |
|---|---|
| **Number** 76142 | **Pieces** 226 |
| **Year** 2020 | **Minifigures** 3 |

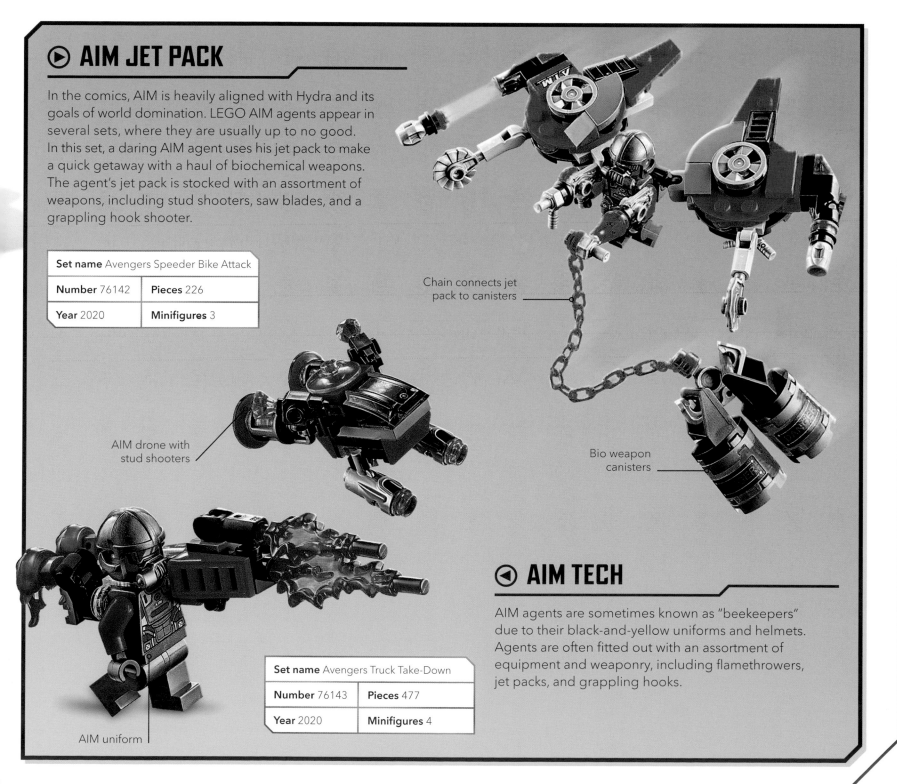

Chain connects jet pack to canisters

AIM drone with stud shooters

Bio weapon canisters

## ◀ AIM TECH

AIM agents are sometimes known as "beekeepers" due to their black-and-yellow uniforms and helmets. Agents are often fitted out with an assortment of equipment and weaponry, including flamethrowers, jet packs, and grappling hooks.

| Set name Avengers Truck Take-Down | |
|---|---|
| **Number** 76143 | **Pieces** 477 |
| **Year** 2020 | **Minifigures** 4 |

AIM uniform

# THOR

Meet the Asgardian God of Thunder! Thor is the son of Odin and brother to Loki. He has the power to manipulate energy and storms, and the strength, endurance, and agility of a god. After being exiled to Earth, Thor finds love with scientist Dr. Jane Foster and joins the Avengers to help save the planet from Loki and his invading Chitauri army. Thor's most famous weapon is the mighty hammer Mjolnir, which can be wielded only by the worthy. He later gains the Stormbreaker axe, which allows him to summon the Bifrost.

## ▼ GOAT BOAT

Thor, The Mighty Thor, Valkyrie, and Korg turn a New Asgard tourist boat into an intergalactic ship with the help of Stormbreaker and two mystical goats. The Viking-style longboat is equipped with everything they need on their journey to Omnipotence City, including a map of Asgard, a boat wrench, and a fire extinguisher.

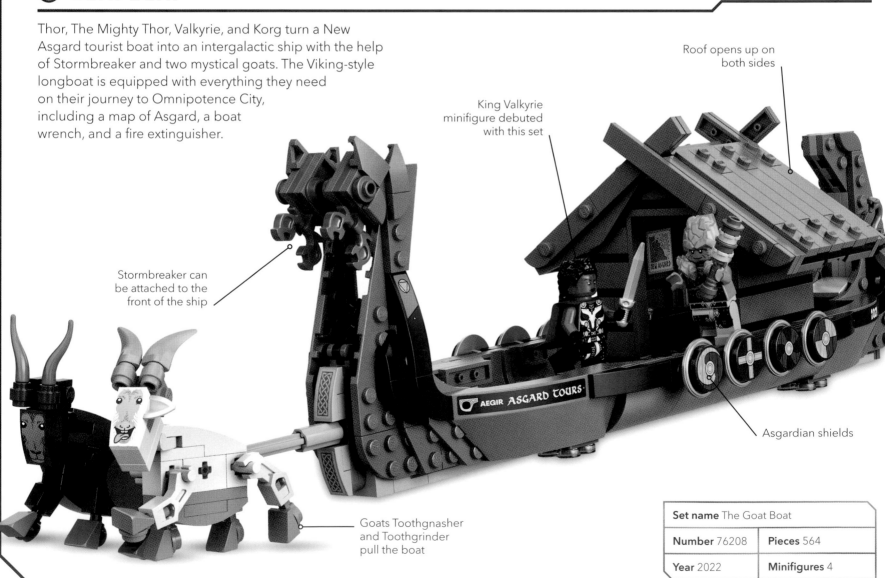

Roof opens up on both sides

King Valkyrie minifigure debuted with this set

Stormbreaker can be attached to the front of the ship

Asgardian shields

Goats Toothgnasher and Toothgrinder pull the boat

AEGIR ASGARD TOURS

| Set name The Goat Boat | |
|---|---|
| **Number** 76208 | **Pieces** 564 |
| **Year** 2022 | **Minifigures** 4 |

## ▶ NEW ASGARD

After the destruction of Asgard and Thanos's successful snap that blipped half of the population of the universe, Thor and his friends Korg and Miek recover on Earth, in New Asgard. Thor passes the time with his new crew, ordering takeout and playing video games in their new house.

Set includes pizza boxes, a TV, and a video game controller

## ▽ THREE THORS

**Thor wears** Sakaaran armor, complete with scabbard and sword, in the gladiator arena where he faces Hulk.

**Thor's Time Suit** makes for comfortable attire during his journey with Rocket to Asgard on a different timeline.

**On his trip** to Nidavellir, where he creates Stormbreaker, Thor's black suit is able to withstand the heat of the weapons forge.

| Set name | Bro Thor's New Asgard | |
| --- | --- | --- |
| **Number** 76200 | | **Pieces** 265 |
| **Year** 2021 | | **Characters** 3 |

**Thor keeps** his long hair much tidier since his return to being a Super Hero. This stylish minifigure comes with a red cape.

## ▶ THE MIGHTY THOR

When New Asgard is attacked by huge, clawed Shadow Monsters, Thor steps up to defend the village. He is joined by Jane Foster, who becomes The Mighty Thor the moment she wields Mjolnir. Together they battle the monsters, which were sent by Gorr as part of his quest to defeat as many gods as he can find.

Claws can pinch together

Mjolnir gives The Mighty Thor superhuman abilities but also weakens her human body

| Set name | Attack on New Asgard | |
| --- | --- | --- |
| **Number** 76207 | | **Pieces** 159 |
| **Year** 2022 | | **Minifigures** 3 |

# ASGARD

Home to Thor, Odin, and Loki, the world of Asgard is one of the Nine Realms. The Asgardians who live there can reach other parts of the galaxy via the Bifrost, which is guarded by the watchful Asgardian Heimdall. When Thor's sister, Hela, returns to Asgard from her banishment, she threatens the lives of all Asgardians. Thor works with Valkyrie, Hulk, Loki, and Heimdall to defeat Hela, and—after the destruction of Asgard itself—to relocate survivors to the village of New Asgard on Earth.

Hela's ten-horned helmet can be removed to reveal her masked, angry face

Hela wields a variety of weapons

Pivoting brick allows Hela's minifigure extra movement

## ▶ HELA

Hela is Odin's firstborn, and serves as the Executioner of Asgard before her father imprisons her. Known as the Goddess of Death, she returns to Asgard after Odin's death, intent on taking the throne. In this set, she comes with a buildable minifigure base, which shows how mighty Thor's sister has become.

**Hela's minifigure** comes with her green cape, a double-sided head piece, a hair piece, and a horned helmet—plus two black power blasts.

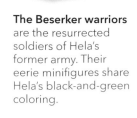

**The Beserker warriors** are the resurrected soldiers of Hela's former army. Their eerie minifigures share Hela's black-and-green coloring.

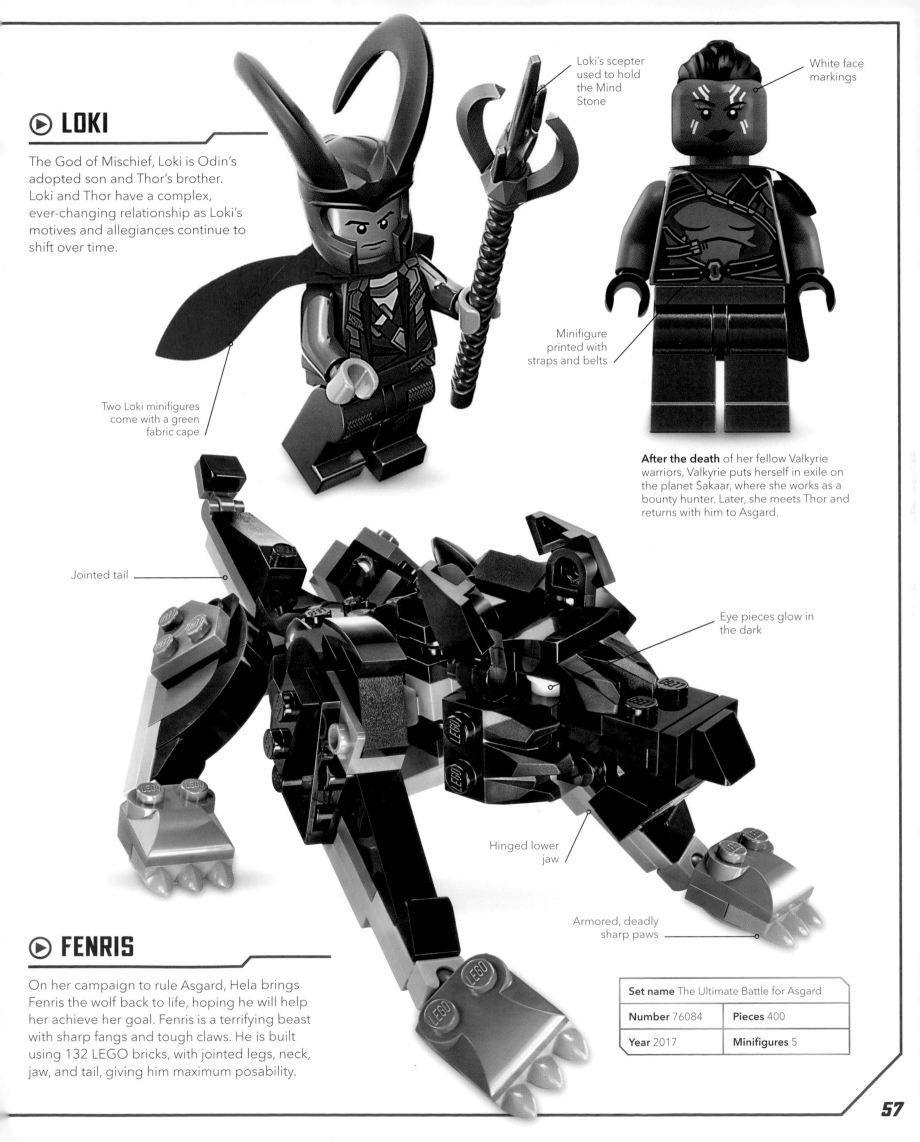

# ▶ LOKI

The God of Mischief, Loki is Odin's adopted son and Thor's brother. Loki and Thor have a complex, ever-changing relationship as Loki's motives and allegiances continue to shift over time.

Loki's scepter used to hold the Mind Stone

White face markings

Minifigure printed with straps and belts

Two Loki minifigures come with a green fabric cape

**After the death** of her fellow Valkyrie warriors, Valkyrie puts herself in exile on the planet Sakaar, where she works as a bounty hunter. Later, she meets Thor and returns with him to Asgard.

Jointed tail

Eye pieces glow in the dark

Hinged lower jaw

Armored, deadly sharp paws

# ▶ FENRIS

On her campaign to rule Asgard, Hela brings Fenris the wolf back to life, hoping he will help her achieve her goal. Fenris is a terrifying beast with sharp fangs and tough claws. He is built using 132 LEGO bricks, with jointed legs, neck, jaw, and tail, giving him maximum posability.

| Set name The Ultimate Battle for Asgard | |
|---|---|
| **Number** 76084 | **Pieces** 400 |
| **Year** 2017 | **Minifigures** 5 |

# BLACK PANTHER

King T'Challa is the Black Panther, protector of the kingdom of Wakanda. Eating a special Heart-Shaped Herb gives T'Challa enhanced senses, speed, and strength. Black Panther's combat suit is laced with vibranium, an almost indestructible metal mined in Wakanda. T'Challa's sister, the scientist Shuri, creates her own Black Panther suit after her brother's death, when she takes on the Black Panther mantle to protect Wakanda from new threats.

T'Challa

Shuri

## ▶ JET PURSUIT

Black Panther follows Iron Man to Siberia in his jet while pursuing the Winter Soldier—an assassin he believes killed his father, T'Chaka. The jet is built in Black Panther's signature colors and holds one minifigure in the cockpit, along with a fire extinguisher—just in case.

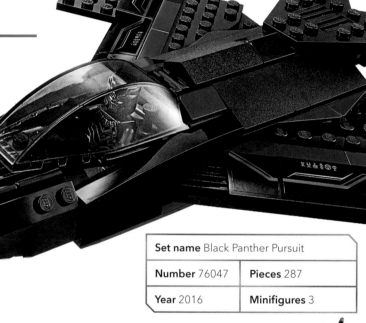

Aerodynamic nose

Stud shooters under wings

| Set name Black Panther Pursuit | |
|---|---|
| Number 76047 | Pieces 287 |
| Year 2016 | Minifigures 3 |

## ▶ ROYAL TALON FIGHTER

The Royal Talon Fighter is Black Panther's personal aircraft. Its cloaking technology allows Black Panther to travel unnoticed outside Wakanda. The ship can also be programmed to fly remotely. In addition to a cockpit, the Talon includes a prison compartment large enough to hold a villain—hopefully Erik Killmonger or Ulysses Klaue, who both come with this set.

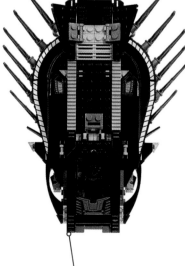

Royal Talon Fighter is in the shape of a mask

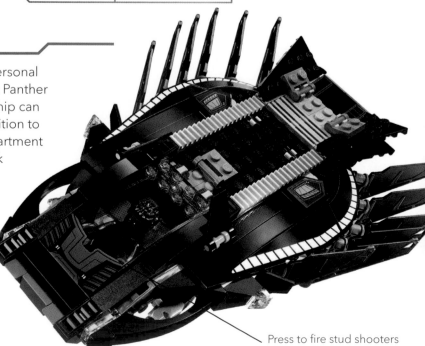

| Set name Royal Talon Fighter Attack | |
|---|---|
| Number 76100 | Pieces 358 |
| Year 2018 | Minifigures 4 |

Press to fire stud shooters

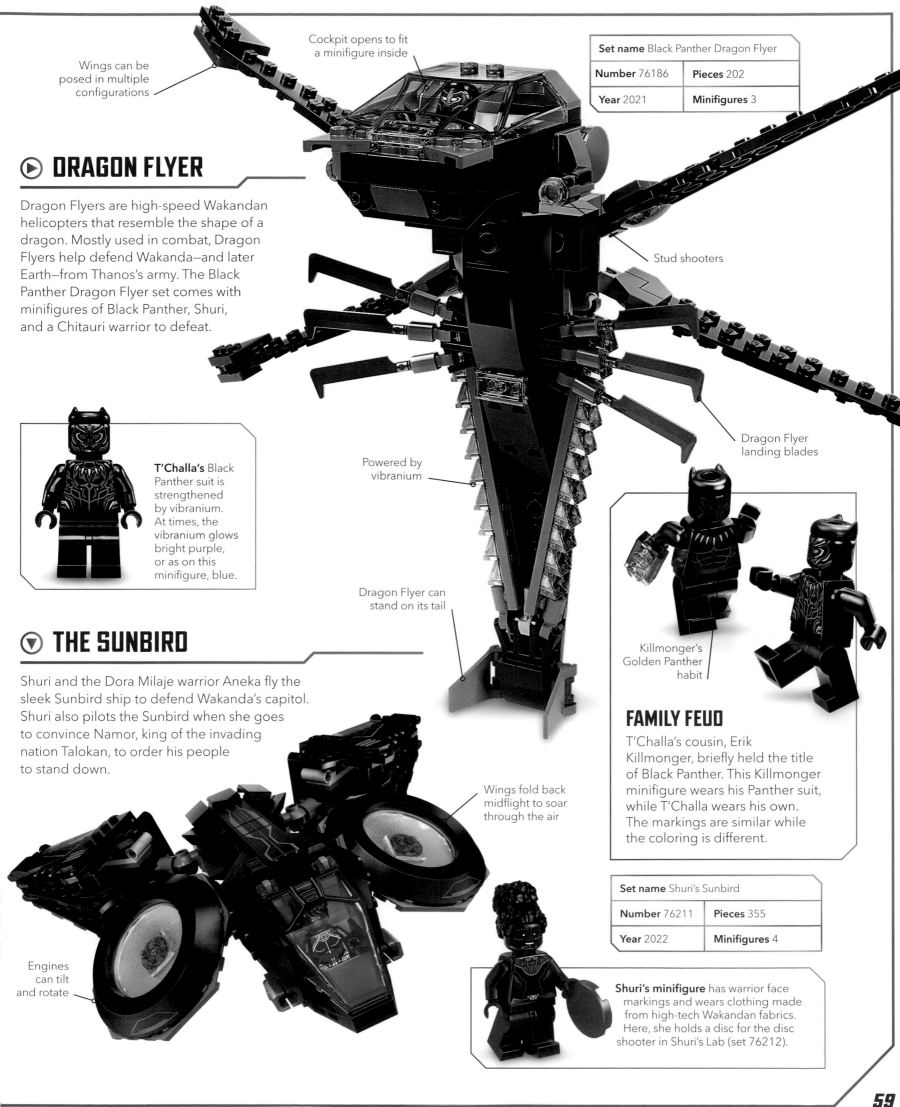

## ▶ DRAGON FLYER

Dragon Flyers are high-speed Wakandan helicopters that resemble the shape of a dragon. Mostly used in combat, Dragon Flyers help defend Wakanda—and later Earth—from Thanos's army. The Black Panther Dragon Flyer set comes with minifigures of Black Panther, Shuri, and a Chitauri warrior to defeat.

Wings can be posed in multiple configurations

Cockpit opens to fit a minifigure inside

Stud shooters

Dragon Flyer landing blades

Powered by vibranium

Dragon Flyer can stand on its tail

T'Challa's Black Panther suit is strengthened by vibranium. At times, the vibranium glows bright purple, or as on this minifigure, blue.

| Set name | Black Panther Dragon Flyer | |
|---|---|---|
| Number 76186 | Pieces 202 | |
| Year 2021 | Minifigures 3 | |

## ▼ THE SUNBIRD

Shuri and the Dora Milaje warrior Aneka fly the sleek Sunbird ship to defend Wakanda's capitol. Shuri also pilots the Sunbird when she goes to convince Namor, king of the invading nation Talokan, to order his people to stand down.

Engines can tilt and rotate

Wings fold back midflight to soar through the air

Killmonger's Golden Panther habit

### FAMILY FEUD

T'Challa's cousin, Erik Killmonger, briefly held the title of Black Panther. This Killmonger minifigure wears his Panther suit, while T'Challa wears his own. The markings are similar while the coloring is different.

| Set name | Shuri's Sunbird | |
|---|---|---|
| Number 76211 | Pieces 355 | |
| Year 2022 | Minifigures 4 | |

**Shuri's minifigure** has warrior face markings and wears clothing made from high-tech Wakandan fabrics. Here, she holds a disc for the disc shooter in Shuri's Lab (set 76212).

# WAKANDA

Wakanda is an African nation that keeps its technological advances hidden from the rest of the world for many years. It is one of the world's largest sources of vibranium, an incredibly strong metal. Scientists use vibranium to create weapons and vehicles. Wakanda's leader, the Black Panther, must defeat any challengers from the other Wakandan tribes before taking the throne.

Top turrets rotate and shoot studs at invading minifigures

Shuri wears vibranium gauntlets

## ▲ DEFENDING WAKANDA

Corvus Glaive and Thanos's Outrider army attack Wakanda on their quest to obtain the Mind Stone from Vision. Black Panther and Shuri defend the walls of their kingdom, doing all they can to keep the precious Infinity Stone out of Thanos's grasp. This set includes a gate that opens and shuts, stud-shooting turrets, and minifigures of Corvus Glaive, an Outrider, and Vision.

| Set name | Corvus Glaive Thresher Attack | |
|---|---|---|
| Number 76103 | Pieces 416 | |
| Year 2018 | Minifigures 5 | |

**M'Baku** is the leader of the Jabari Tribe and the current King of Wakanda. His minifigure wears wooden Jabari armor painted with the face of the Jabari's gorilla god.

**Ironheart** is Riri Williams, a college student who invents a suit similar to Iron Man's armor. Her minifigure wears her Mark 1 armor, which includes a large jet pack.

**Nakia** is a former Wakandan intelligence agent. Her head piece features Wakandan tribal markings, and she holds her signature ring blades.

## ▶ VIBRANIUM MINE

Wakanda's advanced technology is all created with vibranium, a precious and powerful resource mined locally. The vibranium mine itself is operated with high-tech systems and machinery. The mining carts and trains use magnetic energy to glide smoothly above the tracks.

Mining cart tips to pour out vibranium

Unmined vibranium

| Set name Rhino Face-Off by the Mine | |
| --- | --- |
| Number 76099 | Pieces 229 |
| Year 2018 | Minifigures 3 |

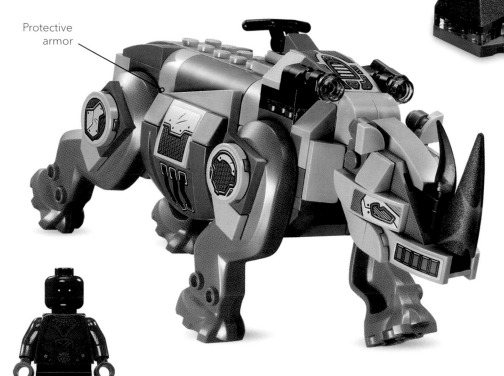

Protective armor

**Wakandan Warrior Okoye** is not a member of the Border Tribe, but the white rhinos know her to be a friend worthy of protection.

## ◀ ARMORED RHINO

The Border Tribe is one of the tribes of Wakanda. It breeds and trains white rhinos for combat in order to protect Wakanda's borders from outside threats. This armored rhino has LEGO armor plating, a seat for a minifigure rider, and two stud shooters for use in the battle between Black Panther and the challenger to the thone, Erik Killmonger.

| Set name Rhino Face-Off by the Mine | |
| --- | --- |
| Number 76099 | Pieces 229 |
| Year 2018 | Minifigures 3 |

## ▶ BATTLE AT SEA

Wakanda isn't the only source of vibranium. The underwater kingdom Talokan is vibranium-rich too, and their king, Namor, wants to join forces with Wakanda against the rest of the world. When Wakanda turns down the offer, Namor leads his people into a sea battle against Wakanda. This set comes with five minifigures ready for battle, including Shuri as Black Panther, Ironheart in her Mark 2 armor, M'Baku, Okoye, and King Namor.

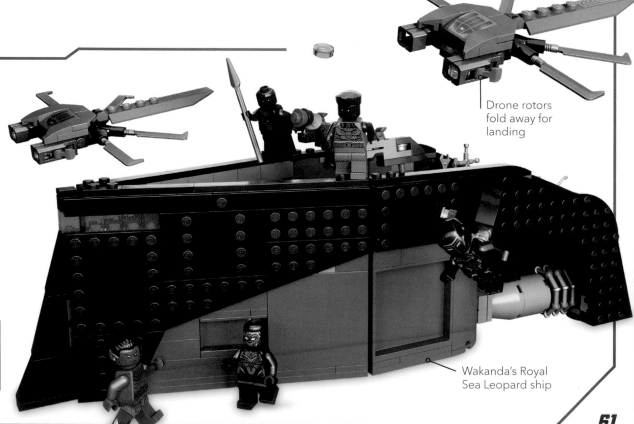

Drone rotors fold away for landing

Wakanda's Royal Sea Leopard ship

| Set name Black Panther: War on the Water | |
| --- | --- |
| Number 76214 | Pieces 545 |
| Year 2022 | Minifigures 5 |

# DOCTOR STRANGE

Before he was a Master of the Mystic Arts, Stephen Strange was a renowned surgeon. After injuring his hands, which threatened to end his medical career, Strange traveled to Kamar-Taj in search of treatment. There, he met the Ancient One, who taught him about magic and The Multiverse. Strange can create portals into other worlds and has learned to use mystical relics such as the Cloak of Levitation and the Time Stone. Doctor Strange, along with other members of the Avengers, defends Earth against harmful magic from other worlds.

Eye of Agamotto amulet

Cloak of Levitation is red with a tall, upstanding collar

## ⦿ SUPER SIDEKICK

Doctor Strange has faced all sorts of villains and scary creatures, so when a terrifying bug monster attacks the workshop at his base, the Sanctum Sanctorum, he isn't too surprised. Luckily, Strange's friend and fellow Master of the Mystic Arts Wong is around to help defeat this interdimensional danger. Wong and Strange defend the Sanctum and all the precious LEGO relics it contains. In case they need more help, Spider-Man and MJ minifigures are included in the set too.

Sticker adds bug-like details

**Once the librarian** of Kamar-Taj, and one of Strange's best friends and allies, Wong is now the Sorcerer Supreme. His minifigure can open portals to other worlds.

Pincers open and shut, trapping Wong!

Vine-like legs

| Set name Spider-Man at the Sanctum Workshop | |
|---|---|
| Number 76185 | Pieces 355 |
| Year 2021 | Minifigures 4 |

# GARGANTOS

Doctor Strange has to make an early exit from ex-girlfriend Dr. Christine Palmer's wedding to save America Chavez, a traveler from another dimension. Chavez, who is still learning to control her powers, is under attack from the giant octopus-like monster Gargantos. The one-eyed creature can climb walls, throw buses, and grab minifigures in its green, winding tentacles.

**America Chavez** meets several versions of Doctor Strange on her travels. Her minifigure wears a jacket covered with pins and patches.

Gargantos has more than a dozen tentacles

Orange eye piece is unique to Doctor Strange sets

Detachable Cloak of Levitation

Protective shield conjured by Doctor Strange

| Set name Gargantos Showdown | |
|---|---|
| **Number** 76205 | **Pieces** 264 |
| **Year** 2022 | **Minifigures** 3 |

**The Ancient One**

**Sinister Strange**

**Karl Mordo**

**Dead Strange**

# MYSTIC MASTERS

There are many LEGO Masters of the Mystic Arts. The Ancient One was the Sorcerer Supreme when Stephen Strange first came to Kamar-Taj for training. Karl Mordo was one of her students. Sinister Strange is an evil version of Doctor Strange, while Dead Strange is a dead version of Doctor Strange, who he possessed while Dreamwalking during his attempt to defeat The Scarlet Witch.

# SANCTUM SANCTORUM

The Sanctum Sanctorum in New York City is one of three bases of the Mystic Arts around the world. Located at the geographical point where powerful energy currents intersect, the New York Sanctum is home to several Masters of the Mystic Arts, such as Doctor Strange and Wong. The Sanctum houses many mystical relics, as well as doorways to other dimensions—including one in the basement that Doctor Strange opened by accident!

Gargantos creature attacks the Sanctum Sanctorum

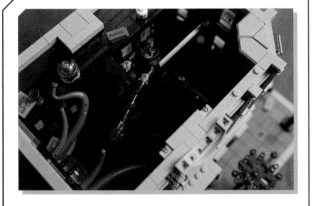

## LIBRARY

The library is stacked with ancient books on the Mystic Arts, as well as a door to different dimensions. A Gargantos creature can be fitted to the wall to set up a dangerous Sanctum invasion scene.

## HIDDEN CHAMBERS

Removing the top section of the grand staircase reveals two hidden rooms. One contains the mystical Time Stone, which gives Doctor Strange the ability to manipulate time.

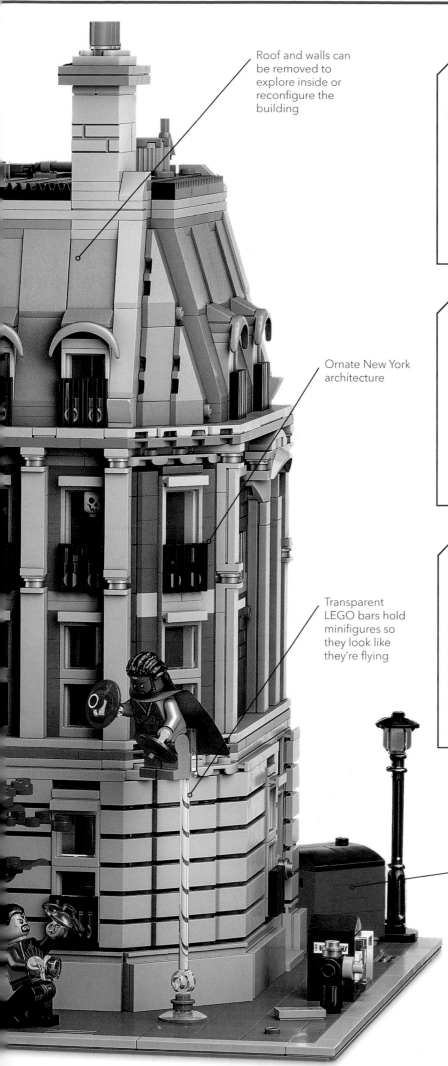

Roof and walls can be removed to explore inside or reconfigure the building

Ornate New York architecture

Transparent LEGO bars hold minifigures so they look like they're flying

Sanctum dumpster

## MULTIPLE STRANGES

The Sanctum's top floor is where Doctor Strange can often be found, gazing out of the iconic Sanctum window. Three versions of Doctor Strange come with this set: Doctor Strange, Sinister Strange, and Dead Strange.

## TOP FLOOR

The top floor of the Sanctum also houses Strange's collection of mystical artifacts, including wall art, weapons, a trunk that contains a scroll, and a hook for the Cloak of Levitation.

## SEEKING STRANGE

Super Heroes know to find Doctor Strange at the Sanctum Sanctorum. Peter Parker comes to ask if Strange can go back in time to prevent Mysterio from revealing Peter's Spider-Man identity.

| Set name Sanctum Sanctorum | |
|---|---|
| **Number** 76218 | **Pieces** 2,708 |
| **Year** 2022 | **Minifigures** 9 |

# BLACK WIDOW

As a child, Natasha Romanoff is separated from her family and trained to be a deadly assassin. Taking the name Black Widow, she later defects to S.H.I.E.L.D. and becomes one of the founding members of the Avengers. Black Widow is a talented spy who can speak many languages, and she is skilled in martial arts. After Thanos wipes out half of the population in the universe, Black Widow takes over the running of the Avengers, coordinating missions and monitoring criminal activity on Earth and beyond.

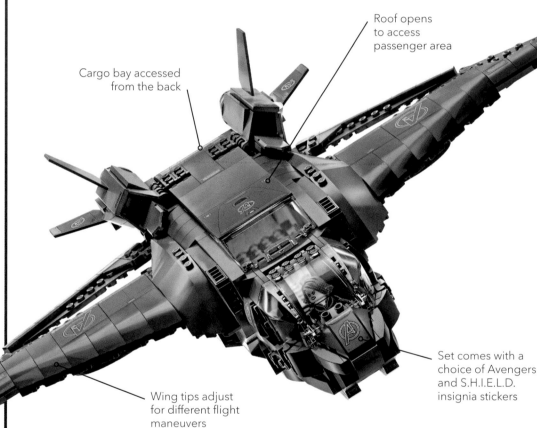

Cargo bay accessed from the back

Roof opens to access passenger area

Wing tips adjust for different flight maneuvers

Set comes with a choice of Avengers and S.H.I.E.L.D. insignia stickers

## ◀ ACE PILOT

Even without super-powers, Black Widow is a valuable member of the Avengers. In addition to her combat skills, she is an expert pilot who can fly all sorts of vehicles. In this set, Black Widow takes the helm of the Avengers' Quinjet and flies it into battle. This Quinjet has adjustable wings and landing gear, so the Avengers on board can be prepared for anything.

| Set name The Avengers Quinjet | |
| --- | --- |
| **Number** 76248 | **Pieces** 795 |
| **Year** 2023 | **Minifigures** 5 |

## ▶ HELICARRIER JET

Black Widow works as a S.H.I.E.L.D. agent in the comics and video games too. In this large LEGO set, she takes flight in an Avengers jet from S.H.I.E.L.D.'s mobile air base, the Helicarrier. Joining Black Widow in the battle against MODOK and an AIM agent are minifigures of Iron Man, Captain Marvel, War Machine, Thor, and Nick Fury.

Adjustable wings

| Set name Avengers Helicarrier | |
| --- | --- |
| **Number** 76153 | **Pieces** 1,244 |
| **Year** 2020 | **Minifigures** 7 |

**Alexei** becomes the Red Guardian after receiving the Super Soldier Serum from the Soviet Armed Forces. He helps train Natasha and Yelena, who think of him almost as a father.

**Black Widow** has been on many Avengers missions. This minifigure wears an advanced tech suit to fly a helicopter in a fierce battle.

**Yelena** is Natasha Romanoff's adopted sister and a former Black Widow assassin. Her minifigure helps Black Widow take on Taskmaster.

**Taskmaster** is a Super Villain who can mimic the fighting styles of her foes. Her minifigure wears a hooded tactical suit and skull-like mask.

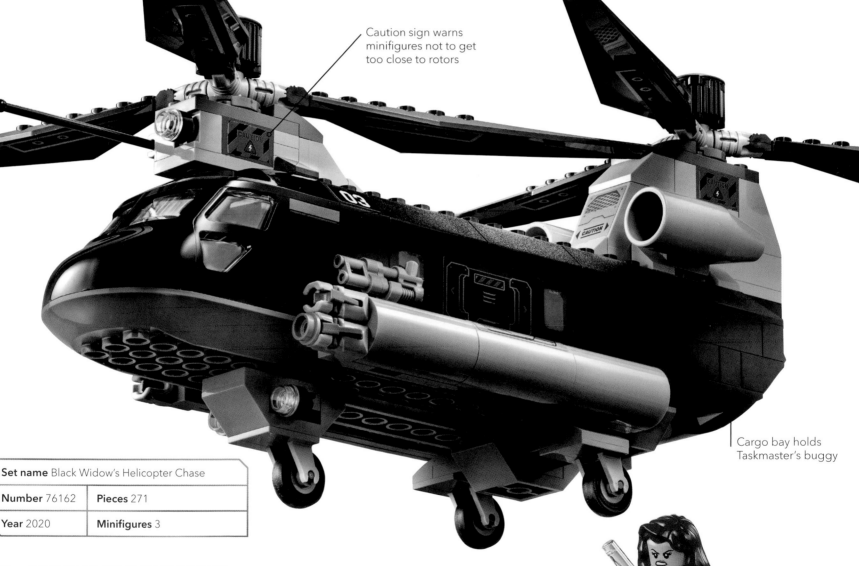

Spinning rotor blades

Caution sign warns minifigures not to get too close to rotors

Cargo bay holds Taskmaster's buggy

| Set name | Black Widow's Helicopter Chase | |
|---|---|---|
| **Number** 76162 | **Pieces** 271 | |
| **Year** 2020 | **Minifigures** 3 | |

## ⊙ ARMED HELICOPTER

Black Widow and Yelena are set on taking out the Red Room, the training program that turns people like themselves into assassins. Standing in their way is Taskmaster, who hunts them down in her armed and very dangerous helicopter. Black Widow and Yelena might be able to escape on their motorcycle, though Taskmaster has a concealed buggy on which she can chase them on the ground.

Sticker adds tech details

# HULK

A gamma radiation serum transforms Dr. Bruce Banner into a giant, green, rage-filled Hulk. Banner spends years fighting to control his Hulk alter ego before turning hero and joining the Avengers. As an Avenger, Hulk helps defeat Loki in the Battle of New York and Thanos in the Battle of Earth. During his time on the planet Sakaar, Banner finds himself trapped in Hulk form. Together with Tony Stark, he creates Smart Hulk, a merging of Banner's mind and Hulk's body. Later, Banner designs a Hulk inhibitor device to keep him in human form.

## ▼ ARENA CLASH

Forced to fight in the Grandmaster's Sakaaran gladiator arena, Thor is relieved to discover that his opponent is his old buddy Hulk—until it becomes clear that Hulk is more focused on winning than rekindling an old friendship. The arena comes with a minifigure launcher and five figures unique to this set: the Grandmaster, Thor, Loki, and a Sakaaran guard minifigure, as well as a super-sized gladiator Hulk "big fig."

| Set name | Thor Vs. Hulk: Arena Clash | |
|---|---|---|
| **Number** 76088 | | **Pieces** 492 |
| **Year** 2017 | | **Characters** 5 |

The Grandmaster's throne falls backward when hit

Loki comes with a golden chalice

Floodlight pillar topples into the arena if pushed

Arena walls can be configured in different ways

**Bruce Banner**

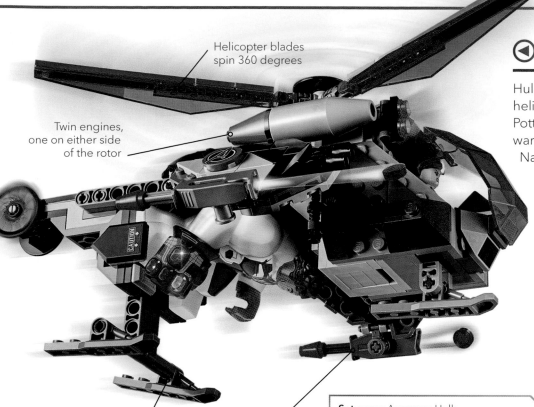

Helicopter blades spin 360 degrees

Twin engines, one on either side of the rotor

Two landing skids at the back

Stud shooters

## ◀ HELICOPTER TRANSPORT

Hulk drops into battle from beneath an Avengers helicopter. He is joined by Black Widow and Pepper Potts, who are ready to take on Thanos's Chitauri warriors. Hulk is in possession of the stone-studded Nano Gauntlet, and hopefully he won't let it out of his sight!

**This Hulk** "big fig" figure wears the Nano Gauntlet, which comes with four of the collectible Infinity Stones.

| Set name Avengers Hulk Helicopter Rescue | |
|---|---|
| **Number** 76144 | **Pieces** 482 |
| **Year** 2019 | **Characters** 5 |

## ▼ HULK VERSUS RED HULK

In Marvel Comics there are lots of Hulks, and they can often be found fighting each other. Whenever such a battle takes place, chaos ensues! In this set, Hulk and She-Hulk take on Red Hulk and Red She-Hulk. Both Hulk teams drive chunky, stud shooter-equipped vehicles that create a big impact. The vehicles launch Hulk and Red Hulk at one another when they collide, taking the smash-up action to a whole new level.

**This smiling She-Hulk** is the first She-Hulk minifigure ever released.

## BRICK FACTS

A unique Hulk minifigure was included in a 27-piece polybag that was originally a Toys "R" Us giveaway in 2015. The bag came with a LEGO buggy for Hulk to smash to pieces.

Adjustable rapid-fire stud shooter

Danger stickers on radioactive containers

| Set name Hulk Vs. Red Hulk | |
|---|---|
| **Number** 76078 | **Pieces** 375 |
| **Year** 2017 | **Characters** 4 |

# CAPTAIN MARVEL

Air Force pilot Carol Danvers gains her super-powers after being exposed to energy from the Tesseract, which houses one of the Infinity Stones. She is taken to Hala by the Kree, who infuse her with Kree blood and erase her memory. Danvers goes by the name Vers during her time with the Kree, but she eventually regains her memories of living on Earth. Realizing the Kree are manipulating her, Danvers takes the name Captain Marvel. Her powers allow her almost unlimited control of cosmic energies. She can fly through space without a suit and has superhuman strength, stamina, and agility.

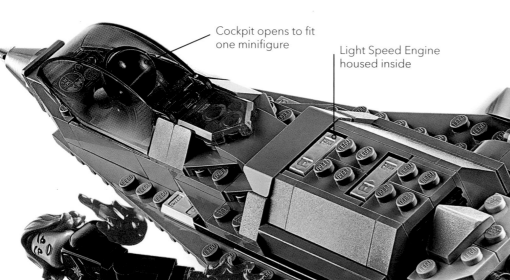

Cockpit opens to fit one minifigure

Light Speed Engine housed inside

The Asis model comes with a display stand

| Set name Captain Marvel and the Asis | |
|---|---|
| **Number** 77902 | **Pieces** 271 |
| **Year** 2019 | **Minifigures** 2 |

## ⬥ NEW POWERS

A San Diego Comic-Con exclusive, this small set shows the moment Carol Danvers gains her super-powers. Danvers and her mentor, Mar-Vell—a Kree scientist living secretly on Earth—are testing a Light Speed Engine that Mar-Vell hopes will end the Kree-Skrull war. When Kree warriors attack the plane, Danvers damages the Tesseract-powered engine to keep the technology out of their hands. Danvers is caught in the explosion and absorbs the Tesseract's energy.

**Maria Rambeau** is Carol Danvers's best friend on Earth. This Air Force pilot is the only Maria Rambeau minifigure to date.

Cosmic blasts

**Talos, a Skrull general,** can shape-shift to look like anyone he's ever come across. His minifigure comes in his true Skrull form, with a two-piece bright green Skrull head.

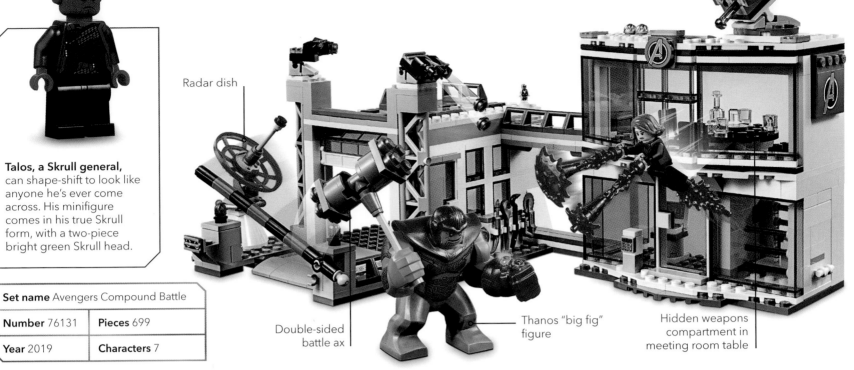

Radar dish

Double-sided battle ax

Thanos "big fig" figure

Hidden weapons compartment in meeting room table

| Set name | Avengers Compound Battle | |
|---|---|---|
| Number 76131 | | Pieces 699 |
| Year 2019 | | Characters 7 |

## GOOSE THE FLERKEN

Goose may look like a cat, but she's actually a deadly alien creature called a Flerken. Goose can attack enemies with large tentacles that shoot from her mouth. She can also store items (such as the Tesseract) in her belly.

## ⊙ AVENGERS COMPOUND

Captain Marvel brings Iron Man and Nebula back to Avengers Compound after their ship stalls in space. This set includes an Avengers meeting room, garage, and helipad—which are all equipped with tools and hidden weapons for when enemies attack. Three special figures are included for the big showdown: "big fig" Thanos, "big fig" Hulk, and an Ant-Man microfigure.

## ▶ AVENJET

The Avenjet transports the Avengers on many of their comic-book missions. The sleek red-and-white jet splits into two vehicles, with the mini-jet detaching from the main one so the Avengers can split up when needed. The main jet holds two minifigures: one in the cockpit and a second beneath the mini-jet. Four unique minifigures are ready for battle in this set—Captain Marvel with an additional masked head piece, Space Captain America, Space Iron Man, and Hyperion. The Thanos "big fig" is also unique to the set.

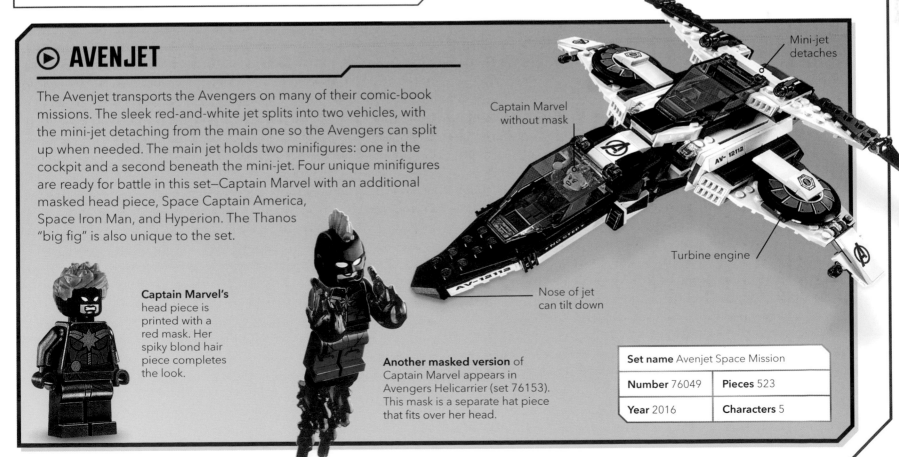

Mini-jet detaches

Captain Marvel without mask

Turbine engine

Nose of jet can tilt down

**Captain Marvel's** head piece is printed with a red mask. Her spiky blond hair piece completes the look.

**Another masked version** of Captain Marvel appears in Avengers Helicarrier (set 76153). This mask is a separate hat piece that fits over her head.

| Set name | Avenjet Space Mission | |
|---|---|---|
| Number 76049 | | Pieces 523 |
| Year 2016 | | Characters 5 |

# HAWKEYE

Before he joins the Avengers, Clint Barton is one of S.H.I.E.L.D.'s most talented agents. Codenamed Hawkeye, Clint is a highly skilled marksman and fighter. Although he has no super-powers, Hawkeye becomes a valued member of the Avengers. He was key to recruiting Natasha Romanoff (Black Widow) into S.H.I.E.L.D., and they continue to work together as part of the Avengers, fighting alongside each other in many battles.

## BRICK FACTS

In set 76126, Hawkeye continues to battle against Thanos and his army. His minifigure wears a Time Suit as it speeds out of the Quinjet to take on some Chitauri warriors.

Minifigure can sit on crossbow platform

Push down to open the sides of the truck

Six-shot crossbow rises up out of the back of the truck

| Set name | Avengers Truck Take-down | |
|---|---|---|
| **Number** 76143 | **Pieces** 477 |
| **Year** 2020 | **Minifigures** 4 |

Windshield opens up

Claw arms on both sides

## ▶ ARMORED TRUCK

Hawkeye and Captain America face off against agents from AIM and their drones. The Avengers' heavily armored truck fits one minifigure in the front cab while another can control the concealed six-shot crossbow that is revealed when the sides of the truck open up.

## ▶ ESCAPE FROM S.H.I.E.L.D.

Hawkeye can aim his bow and arrow with immense precision, but when he is tasked with guarding the Tesseract he fails to see what Loki is up to. The God of Mischief takes control of Hawkeye's mind and uses him to drive the getaway vehicle away from S.H.I.E.L.D. headquarters.

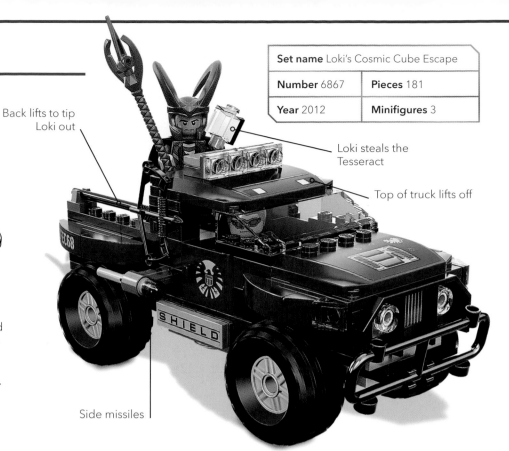

Back lifts to tip Loki out

Loki steals the Tesseract

Top of truck lifts off

| Set name | Loki's Cosmic Cube Escape | |
|---|---|---|
| Number 6867 | Pieces 181 | |
| Year 2012 | Minifigures 3 | |

Side missiles

This Spider-Man minifigure is unique to this set

**Hawkeye's** brainwashed minifigure has this cross expression on one side of his head piece and sunglasses on the other.

## ◀ MOTORCYCLE VERSUS WEBS

A battle at the airport sees Avenger versus Avenger. Spider-Man and Hawkeye are on opposing sides over the Sokovia Accords, which are a government attempt to regulate superhuman activity. Hawkeye fiercely opposes the Accords, and isn't afraid to say so. This set sees Hawkeye use his driving skills and quick reflexes to speed across the tarmac on his purple motorcycle, while Spider-Man tries to catch him with LEGO webs.

Web piece attaches to Spider-Man's hand

Head piece has two expressions, a smirk and a scowl

Rotating turret

Avengers symbol

| Set name | Tanker Truck Takedown | |
|---|---|---|
| Number 76067 | Pieces 330 | |
| Year 2016 | Minifigures 4 | |

## ▶ HYDRA CHASE

The Avengers, including Hawkeye and Thor, reunite to take on Hydra agents and retrieve Loki's scepter. Hawkeye's bow and arrow attaches to the side of the Avengers' 4x4, and a LEGO super-jumper accessory allows both Avenger minifigures to take flight during their pursuit of the Hydra henchman in his off-roader vehicle.

Hydra symbol

| Set name | Avengers Hydra Showdown | |
|---|---|---|
| Number 76030 | Pieces 220 | |
| Year 2015 | Minifigures 3 | |

# ANT-MAN AND THE WASP

Computer engineer and thief Scott Lang agrees to help the scientist Hank Pym retrieve his stolen Ant-Man technology. Lang wears the Ant-Man suit and, with the help of Pym Particles, is able to change the size of his body—from tiny to gigantic! Pym's daughter, Hope Van Dyne, uses the same technology to become The Wasp. Even at insect size, Ant-Man and The Wasp possess superhuman strength. As members of the Avengers, they are able to take down opponents of all shapes and sizes.

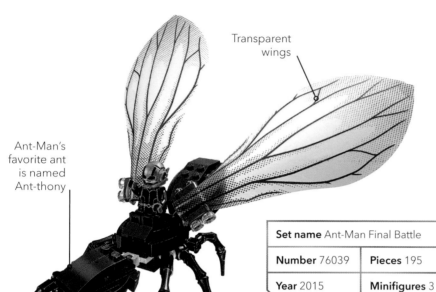

Transparent wings

Ant-Man's favorite ant is named Ant-thony

| Set name | Ant-Man Final Battle | |
|---|---|---|
| **Number** 76039 | | **Pieces** 195 |
| **Year** 2015 | | **Minifigures** 3 |

## ▲ FLYING ANT

Technology in Ant-Man's helmet gives him the ability to communicate with ants. During missions, Ant-Man often rides on the back of an ant, which helps him get quickly from place to place without being noticed by anyone.

**Hank Pym** and his wife, Janet Van Dyne, worked together as Ant-Man and The Wasp until Janet became trapped in the Quantum Realm on a mission.

## ▼ QUANTUM VEHICLE

Hank Pym designs a ship to make the dangerous journey into the Quantum Realm to rescue his wife, Janet Van Dyne. The ship resembles a big-eyed bug and has three engines that enable it to switch easily between launch, hover, and flight modes. Ant-Man and The Wasp's minifigures will need to be careful in the Quantum Realm, because time and space act differently there.

Wing piece also used for Tinkerbell minifigure

**The hooded Ghost** is a young woman named Ava Starr who was overexposed to Quantum energy. The power is slowly killing her.

**Scientist Darren Cross** is Hank Pym's protégé until he steals Pym's tech and uses it to create the Yellowjacket suit.

Robotic arms to grab objects in the Quantum Realm

| Set name | Quantum Realm Explorers | |
|---|---|---|
| **Number** 76109 | | **Pieces** 200 |
| **Year** 2018 | | **Minifigures** 3 |

## ⊽ OLD BROWN VAN

Lang goes on many adventures in his friend Luis's cool van. He once placed a Quantum Tunnel inside the back of the van and then entered the Quantum Realm, only to get trapped there. Luckily, a rat presses the right button five years later, allowing Ant-Man to make his way back. Although the rat does not appear in this set, Ant-Man's return comes at the perfect moment to help the Avengers take on Thanos.

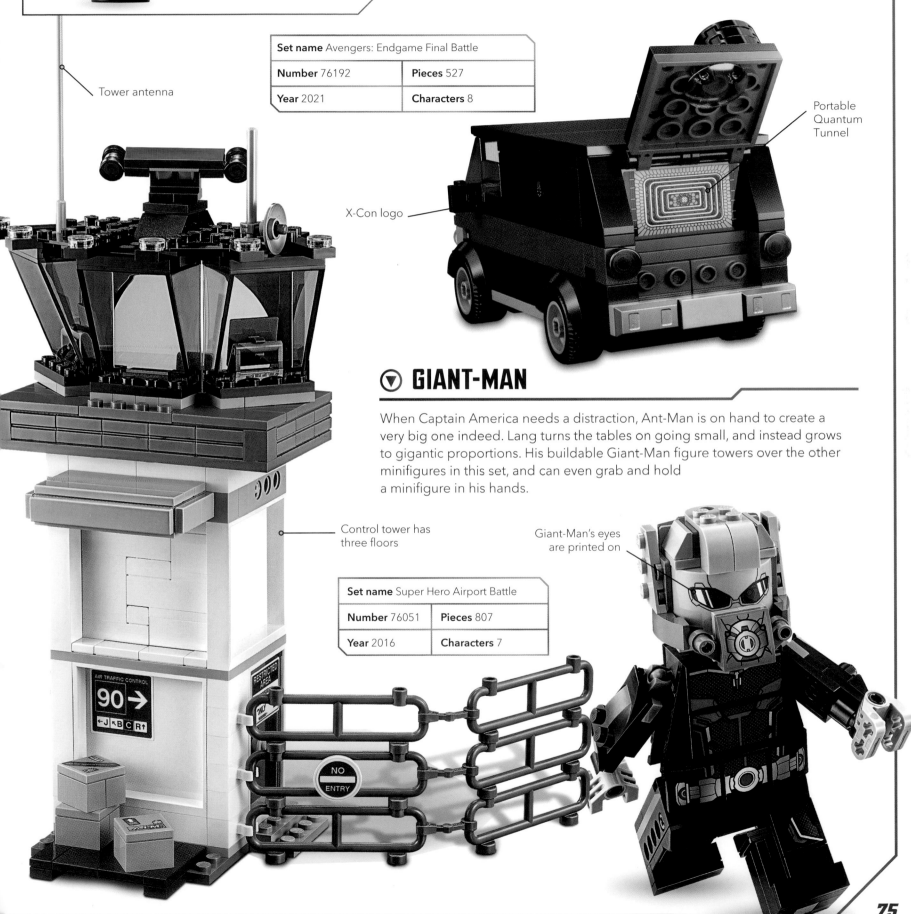

| Set name | Avengers: Endgame Final Battle | |
|---|---|---|
| Number 76192 | | Pieces 527 |
| Year 2021 | | Characters 8 |

Tower antenna

Portable Quantum Tunnel

X-Con logo

## ⊽ GIANT-MAN

When Captain America needs a distraction, Ant-Man is on hand to create a very big one indeed. Lang turns the tables on going small, and instead grows to gigantic proportions. His buildable Giant-Man figure towers over the other minifigures in this set, and can even grab and hold a minifigure in his hands.

Control tower has three floors

Giant-Man's eyes are printed on

| Set name | Super Hero Airport Battle | |
|---|---|---|
| Number 76051 | | Pieces 807 |
| Year 2016 | | Characters 7 |

AIR TRAFFIC CONTROL
90 →
⊢J∢B C R↑

RESTRICTED AREA

NO ENTRY

# WAR MACHINE

James "Rhodey" Rhodes goes from a successful military career to being the Avengers hero War Machine. A long-time friend of Tony Stark, Rhodes dons a full armor suit to become War Machine. The original War Machine armor is an early version of an Iron Man suit. Like Stark, Rhodes wears several versions of the War Machine and Iron Patriot armor, all equipped with heavy firepower that includes swivel mount mini-guns, firing gauntlets, and rocket launchers. Stark helps outfit Rhodes with new technology, as well as leg braces that allow him to walk again following a catastrophic injury.

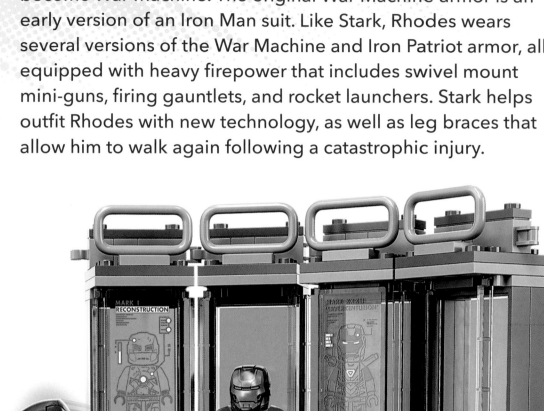

The two floors of the armory can detach from one another

## ◀ ARMORY

The Iron Man armory takes up two stories in the basement of Tony Stark's mansion. This 2022 set is larger than the previous Iron Man Armory set from 2020 (set 76167), which means there is enough space to house a War Machine suit as well as three versons of Iron Man armor. The armory is equipped with a variety of workshop tools, a swivel chair, and holographic display screens.

Iron Man Mark 3 armor

Robotic arm

| Set name Iron Man Armory | |
|---|---|
| **Number** 76216 | **Pieces** 496 |
| **Year** 2022 | **Minifigures** 8 |

Nick Fury enjoys a cup of coffee

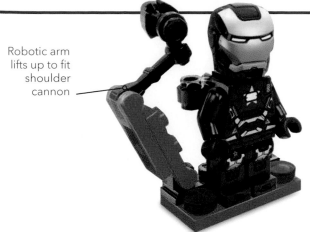

Robotic arm lifts up to fit shoulder cannon

## ◀ IRON PATRIOT

War Machine is known as Iron Patriot when Rhodes wears his red, white, and blue armor. During this time, he works for the US government searching for the criminal known as the Mandarin. The Iron Man patriot minifigure comes in an exclusive polybag set that was only available when preordering the *LEGO® Marvel Super Heroes* video game.

| Set name | Gun Mounting System | |
|---|---|---|
| Number 30168 | Pieces 17 | |
| Year 2013 | Minifigures 1 | |

## ▶ WAR MACHINE BUSTER

War Machine and Ant-Man take on two Outrider warriors with the help of the super-sized War Machine Buster mech that stands over 6in (15cm) tall. The armored mech is fitted with all sorts of tech, including rapid stud shooters and missiles.

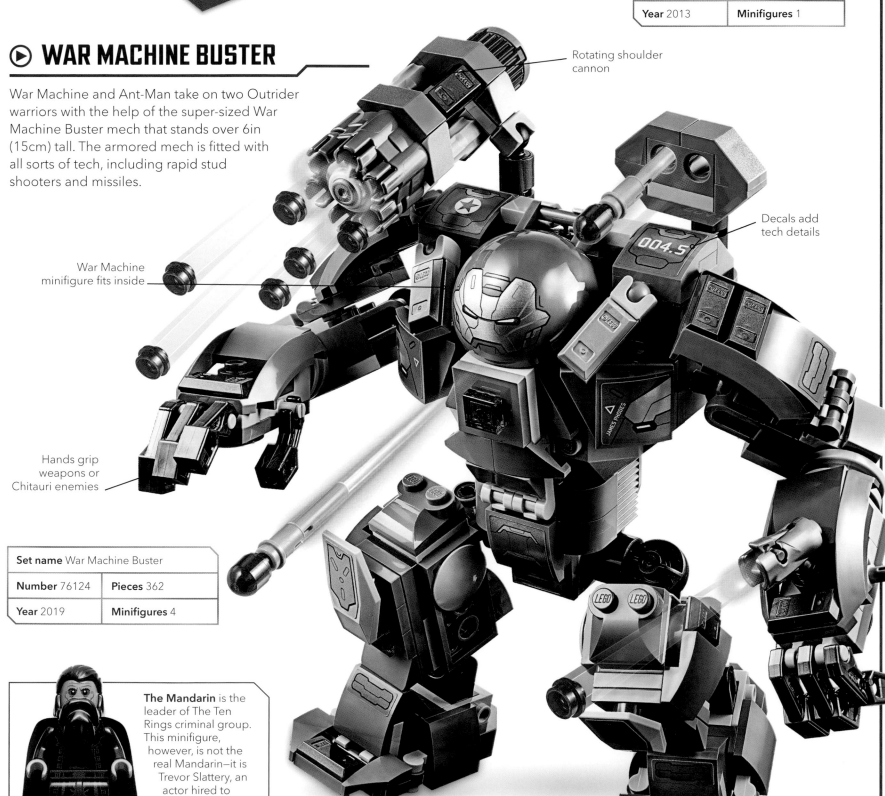

Rotating shoulder cannon

Decals add tech details

War Machine minifigure fits inside

Hands grip weapons or Chitauri enemies

| Set name | War Machine Buster | |
|---|---|---|
| Number 76124 | Pieces 362 | |
| Year 2019 | Minifigures 4 | |

**The Mandarin** is the leader of The Ten Rings criminal group. This minifigure, however, is not the real Mandarin—it is Trevor Slattery, an actor hired to impersonate the group leader.

Posable legs and feet

# VISION

A sentient android, Vision has superhuman strength as well as the ability to fly and move through solid objects. Much of his body is made of vibranium, and his operating system contains the remnants of JARVIS, which allows him to process enormous amounts of information. What makes him truly unique is the Mind Stone, one of the Infinity Stones, which is embedded in his forehead. Unlike Ultron, who was also powered by the Mind Stone and who wanted to end the human race, Vision wants to protect humans, later falling in love with fellow Avenger Wanda Maximoff.

## BRICK FACTS

Vision's minifigure in the 2015 Avengers Quinjet City Chase (set 76032) has a blue circle printed on his forehead to represent the Mind Stone. Later minifigures have a printed yellow circle.

| Set name Tanker Truck Takedown | |
|---|---|
| **Number** 76067 | **Pieces** 330 |
| **Year** 2016 | **Minifigures** 4 |

Transparent fire pieces fold down into the truck

Wind sock triggers barrel explosion when pushed

Twist to open back and start the fire

Front compartment fits one minifigure

## ▲ TANKER TRUCK

When the Avengers are divided over the Sokovia Accords, Vision finds himself up against Captain America at an airport. With a burning LEGO tanker threatening to explode, Vision must choose his side in the heated battle, even if it means standing up to his friends. Vision is accompanied by Spider-Man in this set, while Captain America can rely on help from Hawkeye.

# THE SCARLET WITCH

Before Wanda Maximoff becomes an Avenger, she works with Hydra, seeking revenge against Tony Stark whom she and her brother, Pietro, blame for their parents' death. Following Hydra's experiments with the Mind Stone, Wanda discovers a variety of powers, including telekinesis and the ability to manipulate energy. She joins the Avengers during their battle with Ultron and develops a close relationship with Vision. One of the most powerful Avengers, Wanda later takes the name The Scarlet Witch.

| Set name | Avengers: Endgame Final Battle | |
|---|---|---|
| Number 76192 | | Pieces 527 |
| Year 2021 | | Characters 8 |

## ⊙ BATTLE AT THE COMPOUND

Wanda is unlucky enough to see her beloved Vision die not once but twice! So she is determined to take down Thanos once and for all. She gets her chance in this action-packed set, joining fellow Avengers Iron Man, Captain America, Thor, and Ant-Man in a battle to topple Thanos and his Chitauri warriors.

Satellite dish rotates 360 degrees

Rose-colored blast accessories depict her "scarlet" powers

Chitauri warrior and Thanos can fit inside the compound prison cell

Iron Man's lab

**Wanda's twin brother,** Pietro Maximoff, gains superhuman speed from his exposure to the Mind Stone. He is killed during the Battle of Sokovia.

# FALCON

Sam Wilson is in the Air Force flying an experimental EXO-7 Falcon flight suit. He later leaves the service and meets Steve Rogers when Sam is working with a veterans' support group. The two become fast friends, and when Rogers (as Captain America) needs a wingman for a mission, Wilson is right there by his side. Wilson takes the name Falcon and goes on to join Cap as an Avenger. Wilson's expert piloting skills and the weaponry added to his mechanical wings make him a hard man to track or beat. His wings serve as a shield during battle, while his goggles give him enhanced vision capabilities.

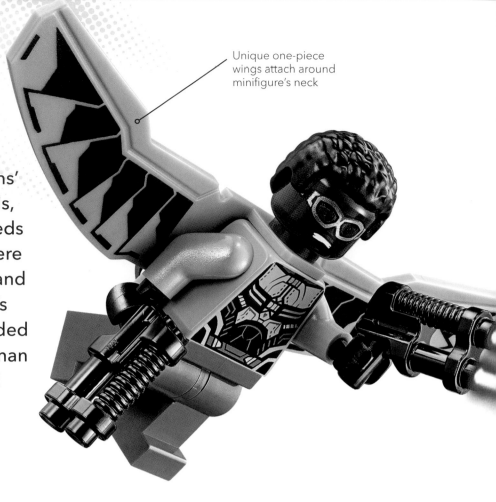

Unique one-piece wings attach around minifigure's neck

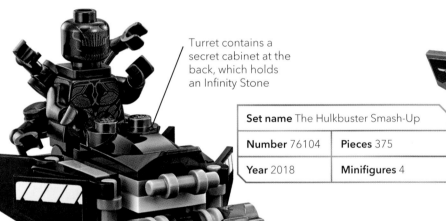

Turret contains a secret cabinet at the back, which holds an Infinity Stone

| Set name The Hulkbuster Smash-Up | |
|---|---|
| Number 76104 | Pieces 375 |
| Year 2018 | Minifigures 4 |

Detachable Redwing drone

Buildable, posable wings

Press springs together to shoot projectile

## ⏺ WAKANDA BATTLE

Falcon's ability to fly gives him an immediate advantage over nonflying foes. In Wakanda, he takes to the skies as he tries to keep back Thanos's army of Outriders. The Outriders might have a lot of arms, but Falcon can swoop through the air! In this battle set, the Outriders are led by Proxima Midnight while Falcon receives ground support from Hulk in his Hulkbuster armor.

**This minifigure** shows Falcon's comic-book look, with red wings and matching red-lensed goggles.

# WINTER SOLDIER

James Buchanan "Bucky" Barnes grows up with Steve Rogers way before Rogers becomes Captain America. During World War II, Barnes is captured by Hydra and experimented on. He spends decades in cryofreeze only to be woken up as the Winter Soldier—a brainwashed assassin with a cybernetic arm and no memory of his past life. Barnes is able to regain control of his mind thanks to Rogers—who risks it all to help his childhood friend—and Shuri. Eventually, the Winter Soldier escapes Hydra's clutches and joins the Avengers to fight against Thanos.

## WHITE WOLF

Barnes is eventually cured of his brainwashing in Wakanda, where he is given the nickname "White Wolf."

## ▽ PANTHER PURSUIT

The Winter Soldier is framed for the bombing attack that killed the once King of Wakanda, T'Chaka. T'Chaka's son, T'Challa (who has taken on the Black Panther mantle), seeks revenge, but Steve Rogers insists on Barnes's innocence. With Black Panther in hot pursuit, Barnes tries to escape on his red LEGO motorcycle.

| Set name | Black Panther Pursuit | |
| --- | --- | --- |
| **Number** 76047 | | **Pieces** 287 |
| **Year** 2016 | | **Minifigures** 3 |

## AIRPORT ESCAPE

Barnes flies a Quinjet to escape a stand-off between the Avengers. He and Cap manage to escape, despite the best efforts of Spider-Man and Black Panther to stop him.

Winter Soldier's gun

Black and silver printed details

Captain America uses shield to protect Barnes

Motorcyle is speedy enough to evade Black Panther

# MS. MARVEL

Pakistani American teenager Kamala Khan loves Super Heroes—and after being exposed to Terrigen Mist (a strange vapor that causes mutations), she becomes one! Kamala can't believe her new shape-shifting powers, which enable her to extend her limbs and change appearance at will. She chooses the name Ms. Marvel to honor her all-time idol, Captain Marvel, and uses her powers to protect her hometown, Jersey City. Even though she has super-powers now, Kamala always makes time for her friends and family.

| Set name | Captain America Jet Pursuit | |
|---|---|---|
| Number 76076 | | Pieces 160 |
| Year 2017 | | Characters 3 |

**The Super-Adaptoid** is built by the evil think tank AIM. It can mimic the appearance and powers of anyone close by.

Arms made of flexible plastic

Transparent red wing piece

Power blasts

### AMAZING ARMS

Ms. Marvel's flexible arms are a single piece of plastic. Pull them through her torso to make one arm longer than the other!

### ⊙ SAVING THE SHIELD

Ms. Marvel teams up with Captain America to help him retrieve his shield from the android Super-Adaptoid. Ms. Marvel's stretchy arms help her evade Super-Adaptoid's power blasts and keep hold of Cap's jet. All three minifigures, including Pilot Captain America, are unique to this set.

# PEPPER POTTS

Pepper Potts plays many roles around her Avenger allies. Starting out as an assistant to Tony Stark, Potts works her way up until she is promoted to CEO of Stark Industries. She also falls in love with the man inside the Iron Man armor. Potts proves her worth on the battlefield after surviving an injection of the gene-altering Extremis serum. She joins the Avengers in the Battle of Earth wearing the Rescue armor.

| Set name Avengers Hulk Helicopter Rescue | |
|---|---|
| **Number** 76144 | **Pieces** 482 |
| **Year** 2019 | **Characters** 5 |

Wings attach as an extra backpack piece around the neck

**Pepper Potts's Rescue** minifigure comes with a hair piece depicting her trademark straight hair for when she takes off her helmet.

Studs shot from Chitauri flyer

Iron Man thruster technology

## BRICK FACTS

There are four Pepper Potts minifigures—two in business suits and two in Rescue armor. But Pepper's head can be fitted onto any Iron Man armor to kick off a new adventure.

## ⊙ BATTLE OF EARTH

During the Battle of Earth, Rescue helps swing Spider-Man and the Infinity Gauntlet out of Thanos's reach. The Infinity Gauntlet is worn by Hulk, who joins Rescue in this set as they try to defeat hordes of Chitauri soldiers. Rescue's minifigure armor includes a helmet and detachable armored wings.

# NICK FURY

S.H.I.E.L.D. agent Nick Fury doesn't believe in Super Heroes or aliens—until he meets Captain Marvel! His first adventure with her gives him the idea to recruit a team of "Avengers" to defend Earth and sets him on the path to becoming director of S.H.I.E.L.D. Though he has no super-powers of his own, Nick is a strong leader, and the Avengers rely on his help more than once, and consider him a trusted friend and ally.

Trademark eyepatch

Space in the back for Goose the cat

Four missiles fire at once

S.H.I.E.L.D. insignia

Cockpit holds two minifigures

**Young Nick's minifigure** wears a gun holster but doesn't feature an eyepatch, since he had two working eyes when he first met Captain Marvel.

| Set name Captain Marvel and The Skrull Attack | |
| --- | --- |
| **Number** 76127 | **Pieces** 307 |
| **Year** 2019 | **Minifigures** 3 |

## ◤ QUADJET ESCAPE

Nick Fury meets Captain Marvel when she fights alien Skrulls on Earth. He unwittingly leads the Skrull leader, Talos, to Marvel's location, before helping her escape in a S.H.I.E.L.D. Quadjet. The set comes with a Talos minifigure, who later helps Nick and Marvel upgrade the Quadjet so it can travel to outer space.

## NICK OR NOT?

Nick is always thinking up new ways to help out the Avengers. While you can't tell from his minifigures, sometimes, he lets a shape-shifting Skrull stand in for him, so he can be in two places at once!

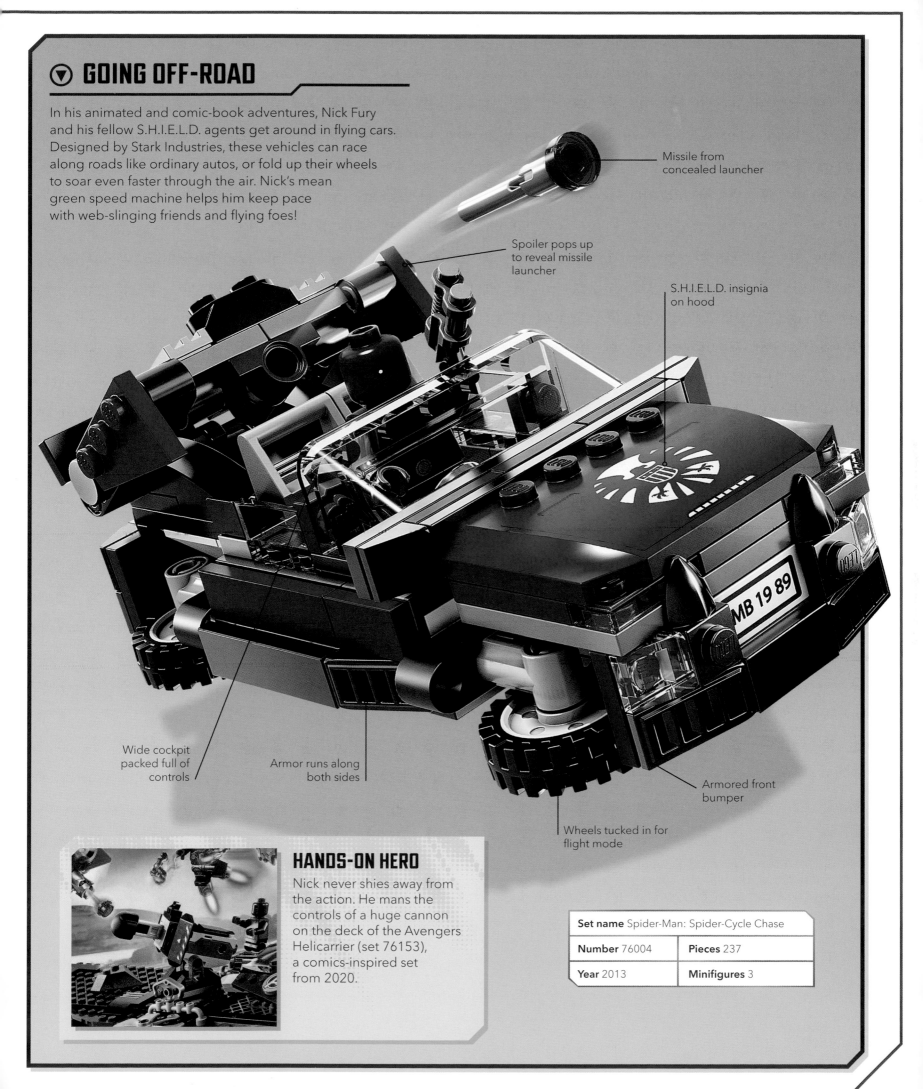

## ⊙ GOING OFF-ROAD

In his animated and comic-book adventures, Nick Fury and his fellow S.H.I.E.L.D. agents get around in flying cars. Designed by Stark Industries, these vehicles can race along roads like ordinary autos, or fold up their wheels to soar even faster through the air. Nick's mean green speed machine helps him keep pace with web-slinging friends and flying foes!

Missile from concealed launcher

Spoiler pops up to reveal missile launcher

S.H.I.E.L.D. insignia on hood

Wide cockpit packed full of controls

Armor runs along both sides

Armored front bumper

Wheels tucked in for flight mode

### HANDS-ON HERO

Nick never shies away from the action. He mans the controls of a huge cannon on the deck of the Avengers Helicarrier (set 76153), a comics-inspired set from 2020.

| Set name | Spider-Man: Spider-Cycle Chase | |
|---|---|---|
| Number 76004 | | Pieces 237 |
| Year 2013 | | Minifigures 3 |

# S.H.I.E.L.D.

The Strategic Homeland Intervention, Enforcement, and Logistics Division (S.H.I.E.L.D.) was set up more than 70 years ago to defend the US against enemies with advanced technology. Today, its main mission is to protect Earth from Super Villains and threats from other worlds. S.H.I.E.L.D. operatives tend to be brave humans without super-powers, but the organization also works closely with the Avengers. S.H.I.E.L.D.'s most famous agent is Nick Fury, but its ranks boast many other leaders and heroes.

**Agent Hill's minifigure** wears a crisp S.H.I.E.L.D. uniform when she co-commands the division's flying headquarters, the S.H.I.E.L.D. Helicarrier (set 76042).

## ▶ DEPUTY DIRECTOR HILL

When Nick Fury is in charge of S.H.I.E.L.D., Maria Hill is his trusted second in command. She is by his side when the Chitauri attack New York City and when Hydra take over S.H.I.E.L.D.

One of Mysterio's many drones

Maria Hill in casual clothes

| Set name Spider-Man and the Museum Break-In | |
| --- | --- |
| Number 40343 | Pieces 49 |
| Year 2019 | Minifigures 3 |

## ▼ AGENT COULSON

Phillip J. Coulson is one of S.H.I.E.L.D.'s most experienced operatives and has worked with his friend Nick Fury for many years. His prized possession is Lola, a sleek sports car from the 1960s. Coulson uses S.H.I.E.L.D. technology to turn the classic corvette into a flying machine, and the LEGO version can tranform just as smoothly. The name Lola refers to the vehicle's new status as a Levitating Over Land Automobile!

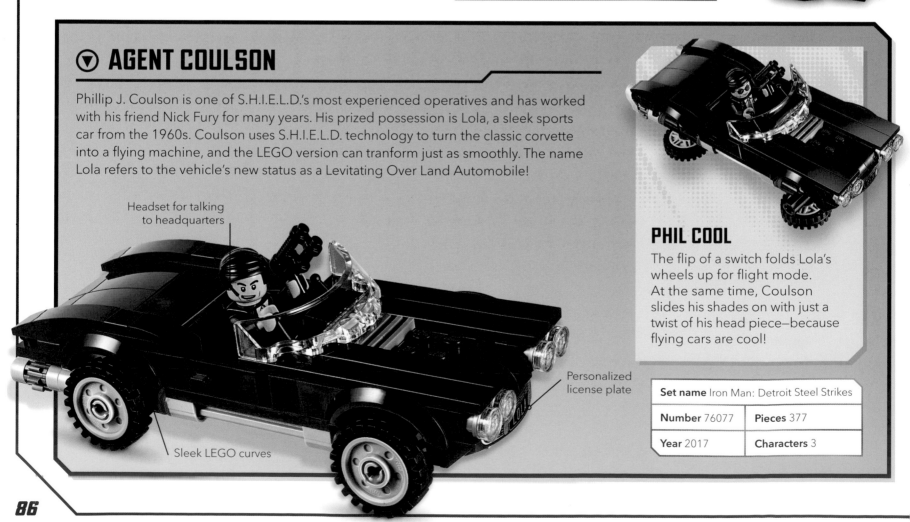

Headset for talking to headquarters

### PHIL COOL

The flip of a switch folds Lola's wheels up for flight mode. At the same time, Coulson slides his shades on with just a twist of his head piece—because flying cars are cool!

Personalized license plate

Sleek LEGO curves

| Set name Iron Man: Detroit Steel Strikes | |
| --- | --- |
| Number 76077 | Pieces 377 |
| Year 2017 | Characters 3 |

**Peggy Carter** is the co-founder of S.H.I.E.L.D., but in an alternative reality, she becomes the world's first Avenger, instead of Captain America!

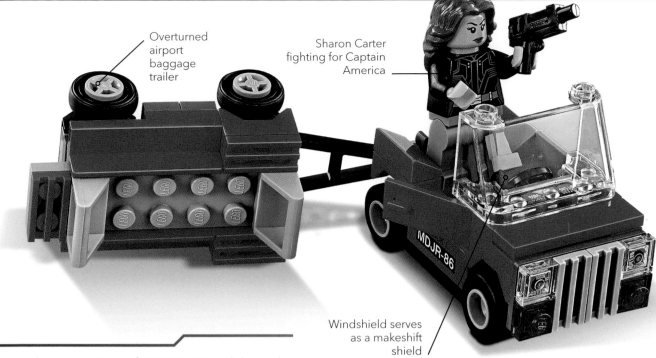

Overturned airport baggage trailer

Sharon Carter fighting for Captain America

Windshield serves as a makeshift shield

# ▶ AGENT 13

Codenamed Agent 13, Sharon Carter is the great-niece of S.H.I.E.L.D.'s celebrated co-founder, Peggy Carter. Though she dearly loved her great-aunt, Sharon didn't want special treatment as a S.H.I.E.L.D. operative, so she kept her family connection a secret. Like Peggy decades before, Sharon is a close friend of Captain America, and she sides with him over S.H.I.E.L.D. in the Avengers' civil war.

| Set name | Super Hero Airport Battle | |
|---|---|---|
| **Number** 76051 | | **Pieces** 807 |
| **Year** 2016 | | **Characters** 7 |

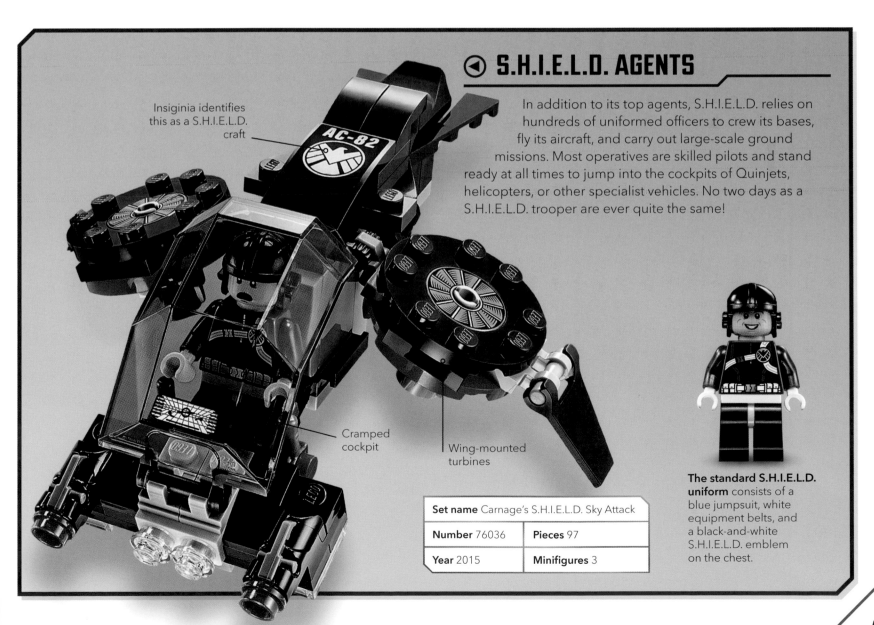

Insiginia identifies this as a S.H.I.E.L.D. craft

AC-82

Cramped cockpit

Wing-mounted turbines

# ◀ S.H.I.E.L.D. AGENTS

In addition to its top agents, S.H.I.E.L.D. relies on hundreds of uniformed officers to crew its bases, fly its aircraft, and carry out large-scale ground missions. Most operatives are skilled pilots and stand ready at all times to jump into the cockpits of Quinjets, helicopters, or other specialist vehicles. No two days as a S.H.I.E.L.D. trooper are ever quite the same!

**The standard S.H.I.E.L.D. uniform** consists of a blue jumpsuit, white equipment belts, and a black-and-white S.H.I.E.L.D. emblem on the chest.

| Set name | Carnage's S.H.I.E.L.D. Sky Attack | |
|---|---|---|
| **Number** 76036 | | **Pieces** 97 |
| **Year** 2015 | | **Minifigures** 3 |

# THE HELICARRIER

S.H.I.E.L.D.'s most impressive base is the Helicarrier, a vast, flying aircraft carrier that can operate at sea or in the air. When the craft was badly damaged in an attack by Loki, S.H.I.E.L.D. built three more Helicarriers. However, when Hydra tries to take control of the fleet, Captain America stops them by causing the Helicarriers to shoot each other down. Later, Nick Fury has the first Helicarrier repaired and uses it to save many lives in the battle against Ultron.

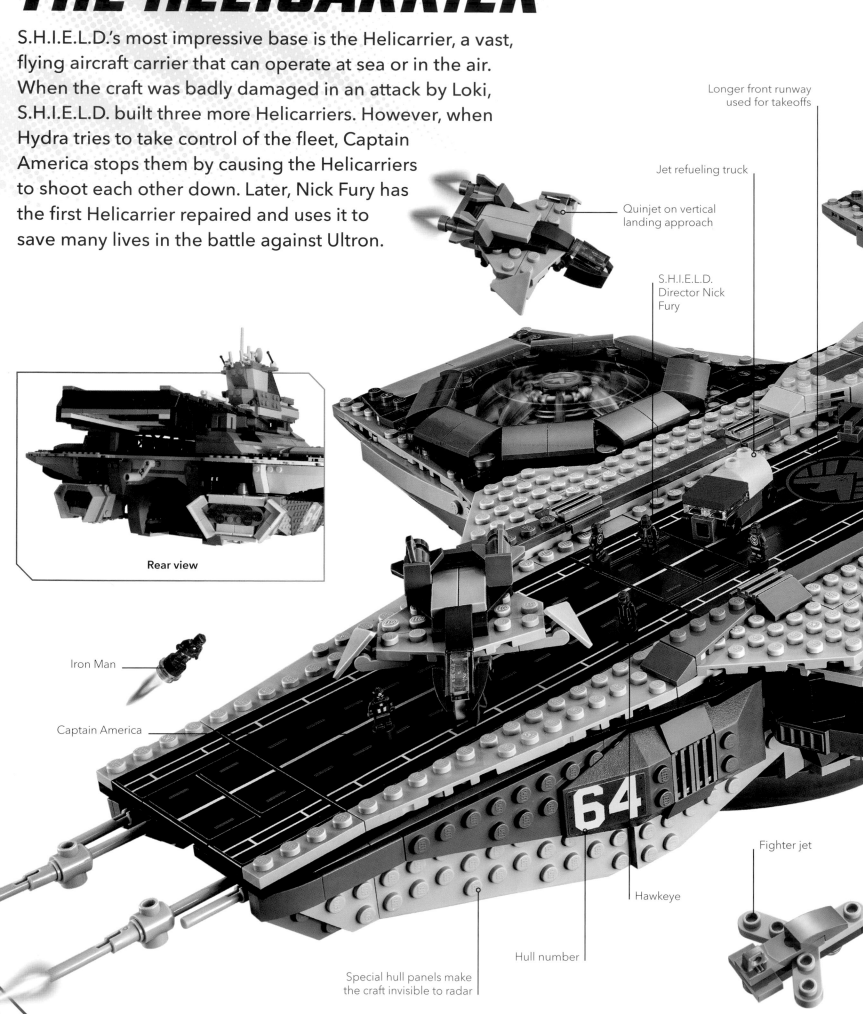

Longer front runway used for takeoffs

Jet refueling truck

Quinjet on vertical landing approach

S.H.I.E.L.D. Director Nick Fury

**Rear view**

Iron Man

Captain America

Fighter jet

Hawkeye

Hull number

Special hull panels make the craft invisible to radar

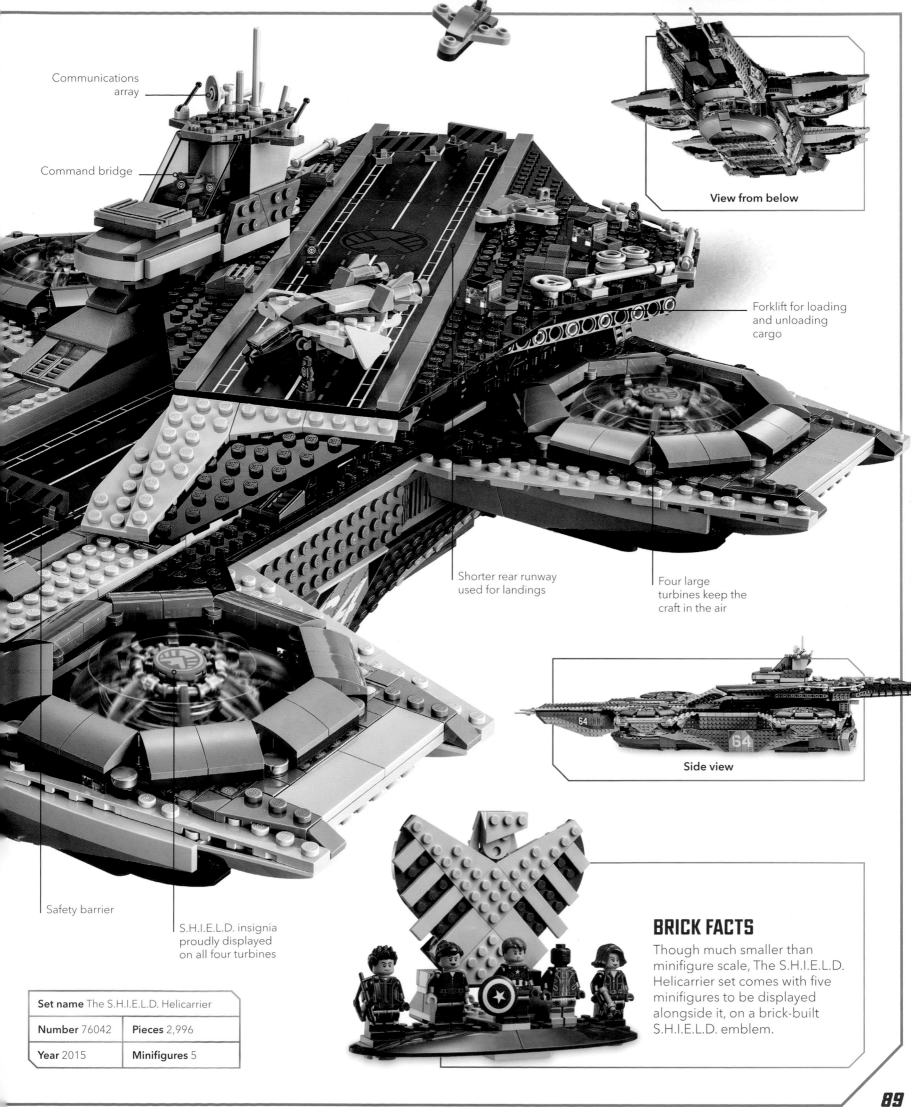

Communications array

Command bridge

**View from below**

Forklift for loading and unloading cargo

Shorter rear runway used for landings

Four large turbines keep the craft in the air

**Side view**

Safety barrier

S.H.I.E.L.D. insignia proudly displayed on all four turbines

## BRICK FACTS

Though much smaller than minifigure scale, The S.H.I.E.L.D. Helicarrier set comes with five minifigures to be displayed alongside it, on a brick-built S.H.I.E.L.D. emblem.

| Set name | The S.H.I.E.L.D. Helicarrier | |
|---|---|---|
| Number | 76042 | Pieces 2,996 |
| Year | 2015 | Minifigures 5 |

# THE QUINJET

S.H.I.E.L.D. develops the powerful Quinjet as a successor to its experimental Quadjet. The unique Quinjet design combines five jet thrusters for super-fast speeds with wing-mounted turbines for hovering and maneuvering abilities like a helicopter's. The Avengers use their own, larger version of the Quinjet, which boasts advanced autopilot and stealth capabilities, plus extra room for passengers and cargo. Quinjets are designed for use within Earth's atmosphere, though Hulk uses one to travel to another planet!

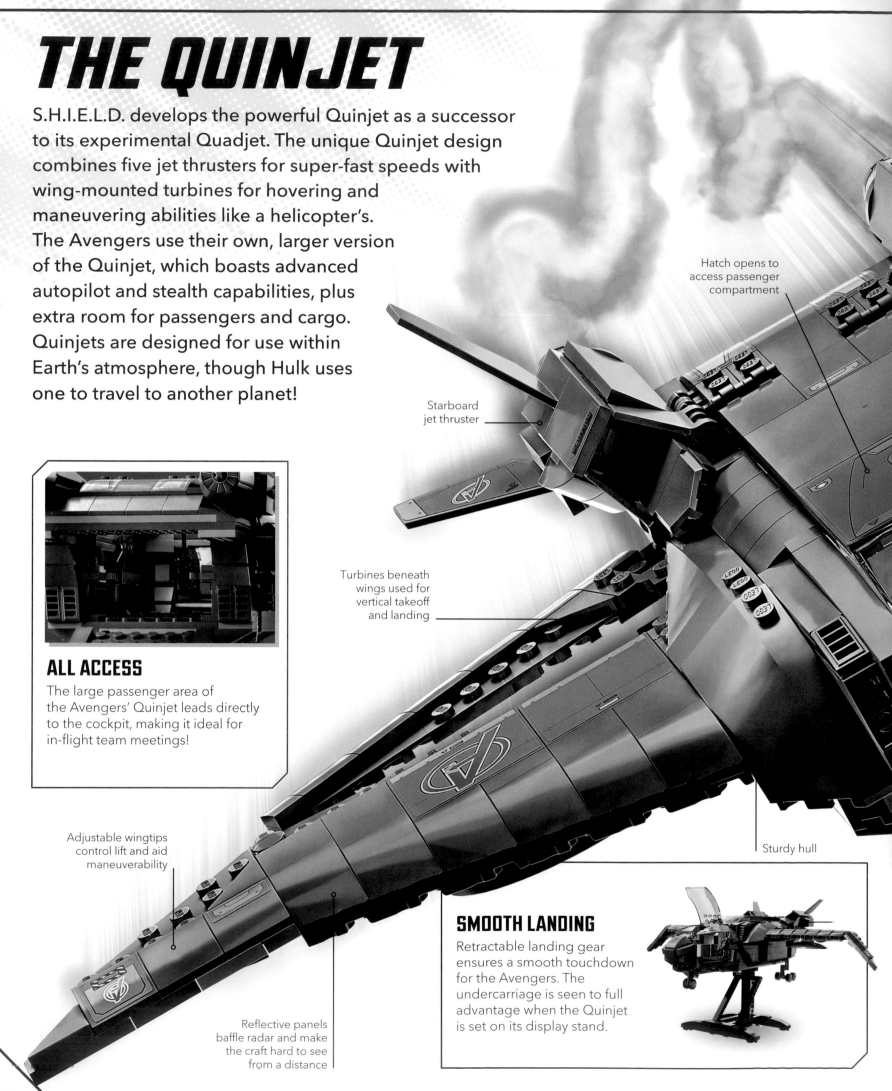

Hatch opens to access passenger compartment

Starboard jet thruster

Turbines beneath wings used for vertical takeoff and landing

## ALL ACCESS

The large passenger area of the Avengers' Quinjet leads directly to the cockpit, making it ideal for in-flight team meetings!

Adjustable wingtips control lift and aid maneuverability

Reflective panels baffle radar and make the craft hard to see from a distance

Sturdy hull

## SMOOTH LANDING

Retractable landing gear ensures a smooth touchdown for the Avengers. The undercarriage is seen to full advantage when the Quinjet is set on its display stand.

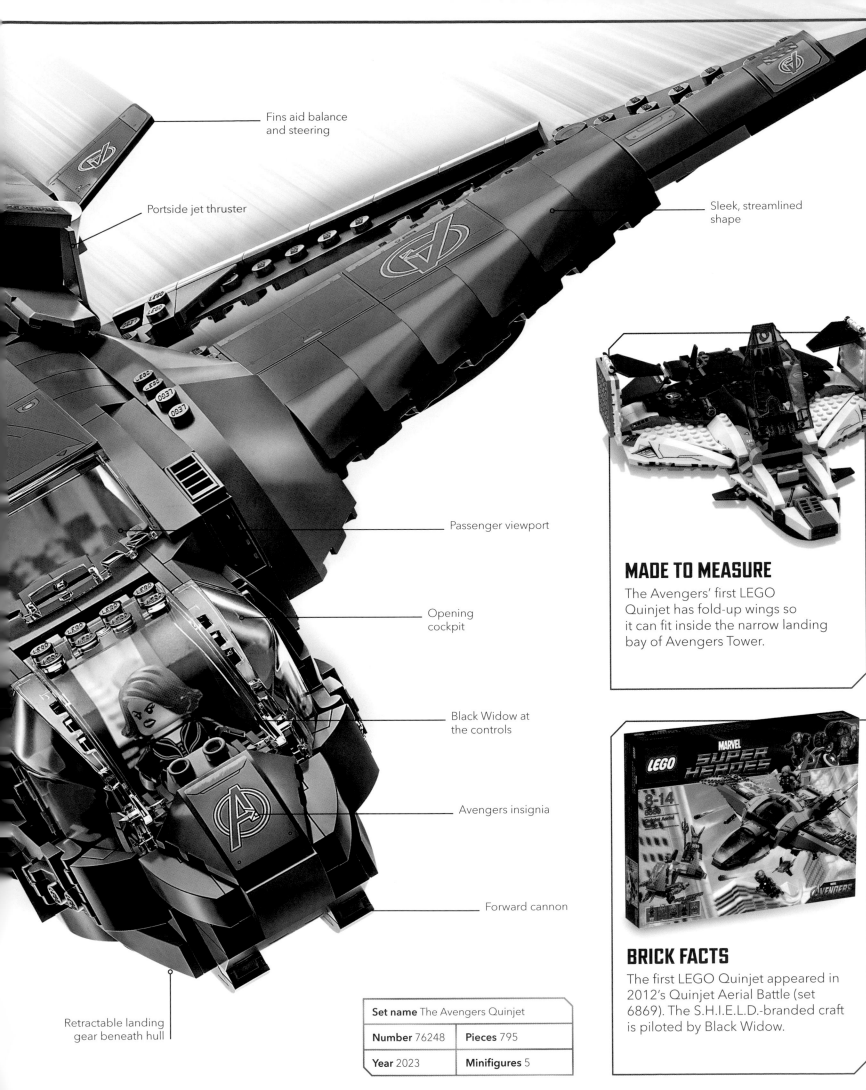

Fins aid balance
and steering

Portside jet thruster

Sleek, streamlined
shape

Passenger viewport

## MADE TO MEASURE

The Avengers' first LEGO
Quinjet has fold-up wings so
it can fit inside the narrow landing
bay of Avengers Tower.

Opening
cockpit

Black Widow at
the controls

Avengers insignia

## BRICK FACTS

The first LEGO Quinjet appeared in
2012's Quinjet Aerial Battle (set
6869). The S.H.I.E.L.D.-branded craft
is piloted by Black Widow.

Forward cannon

Retractable landing
gear beneath hull

| Set name The Avengers Quinjet | |
| --- | --- |
| **Number** 76248 | **Pieces** 795 |
| **Year** 2023 | **Minifigures** 5 |

# THANOS

Thanos is the Avengers' greatest enemy. When his home planet, Titan, is doomed by a lack of resources, he decides that the universe would be a better place with only half as many people in it. In pursuit of this terrible dream, he plunders countless worlds in search of the hugely powerful Infinity Stones. With all six stones in his possession, Thanos will be able to remove half of life in the universe with a simple snap of his fingers!

Most LEGO Thanos figures are "big fig" versions

## ▶ SANCTUARY II

Thanos travels the universe in an enormous ship called the *Sanctuary II*. The first thing he does when he comes to Earth is attack the Avengers' base using the weapons on *Sanctuary II*. Though Thanos can cause significant damage using its missiles alone, he prefers to unleash his Chitauri and Outrider armies from the vessel's huge interior.

| Set name | Sanctuary II: Endgame Battle | |
|---|---|---|
| Number 76237 | Pieces 322 | |
| Year 2021 | Minifigures 3 | |

### BRICK FACTS

While most sets feature an oversized Thanos "big fig," Sanctuary II: Endgame Battle includes a minifigure version that fits inside the ship.

Hull is more like rock than metal

Missile launchers

Smaller ships can dock beneath these massive wings

Wingtips are more than 2.5 miles (4km) apart!

# INFINITY GAUNTLET

Thanos gathers the six Infinity Stones from around the universe and adds them to a special gauntlet, combining their powers in a single weapon. The stones are the blue Space Stone, yellow Mind Stone, red Reality Stone, purple Power Stone, green Time Stone, and orange Soul Stone. LEGO Infinity Stones can be found in various LEGO sets, but there are only two sets that come with all six: The 2021 Avengers Advent Calendar (set 76196) and Thor's Hammer (set 76209). Unfortunately for Thanos, his "big fig" doesn't appear in either of those sets!

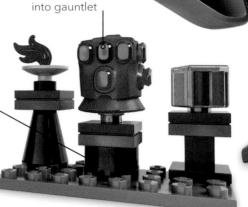

Thanos from set 76107 would do anything to possess all six stones!

Stones clip into gauntlet

| Set name Thor's Hammer | |
| --- | --- |
| Number 76209 | Pieces 979 |
| Year 2022 | Minifigures 1 |

Gauntlet stand

Golden details match Thanos's armor

Force field generators

## NANO GAUNTLET

To combat Thanos, Tony Stark builds his own version of the Infinity Gauntlet, using the same nanotechnology as his Iron Man suits.

Space Iron Man

| Set name Avenjet Space Mission | |
| --- | --- |
| Number 76049 | Pieces 523 |
| Year 2016 | Characters 5 |

Command center and throne room

## THANOS IN SPACE

Thanos wears jet-propelled boots and fights space-suited versions of Iron Man and Captain America in Avenjet Space Mission, a set inspired by the Avengers' animated adventures. This version of the super-strong Titan doesn't want to wipe out half of the universe—he simply wants to rule everyone in it!

Missile launchers built into jet boots

# THE CHILDREN OF THANOS

Thanos's most trusted generals are his adopted children. Taken at a young age from worlds he has conquered, they are raised to be fiercely loyal to the power-hungry Titan and trained as ruthless warriors and master tacticians. As adults, they become leaders of Thanos's army, spreading fear and destruction across the galaxy. Thanos unleashes his children on Earth to steal two of the Infinity Stones, and he later sends them to collect another stone in Wakanda.

Obsidian towers over Doctor Strange

Tough, reptilian skin

Weapon is simple but effective

## ◀ CULL OBSIDIAN

The strongest of Thanos's children, Cull Obsidian wields a huge pair of hammers linked by a chain. When Thanos sends him to New York City in search of the Time Stone, he proves a match for Doctor Strange, Iron Man, and Spider-Man combined, before Wong sends him through a trans-dimensional portal into the Arctic. His LEGO "big fig" reflects his impressive size.

Protective shield

Time Stone

### STRANGE STONE

Doctor Strange is responsible for the safety of the Time Stone on Earth, and uses it to see possible futures. This places him at risk from the Children of Thanos.

| Set name Sanctum Sanctorum Showdown | |
|---|---|
| **Number** 76108 | **Pieces** 1,004 |
| **Year** 2018 | **Characters** 5 |

Pale green skin

Elegantly armored tunic

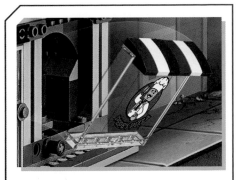

## BRICK FACTS

Action features in Sanctum Sanctorum Showdown include windows that can be knocked out as the Children of Thanos attack the building.

Iron Man in Mark 50 armor

| Set name | Sanctum Sanctorum Showdown | |
|---|---|---|
| **Number** 76108 | **Pieces** 1,004 | |
| **Year** 2018 | **Characters** 5 | |

## ⊙ EBONY MAW

Ebony Maw's immense telekinetic powers allow him to control objects with his mind alone. In battle, he can create chaos around himself without ever moving a muscle! He also proclaims his master's infinite majesty wherever he goes—telling those about to be conquered that they are lucky to be part of Thanos's grand plan!

Hulkish rage in Bruce Banner's eyes

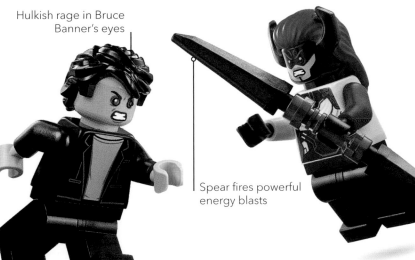

## ◉ PROXIMA MIDNIGHT

Proxima Midnight takes delight in defeating her enemies. Tasked by Thanos to take the Mind Stone from Vision's head, Proxima and Corvus Glaive hunt him down in Edinburgh, Scotland, but they fail. She tries again in Wakanda, where she and her fellow Children of Thanos lead a massive assault on Black Panther's kingdom, facing off against a team of Avengers and the Wakandan army.

Spear fires powerful energy blasts

| Set name | The Hulkbuster Smash-Up | |
|---|---|---|
| **Number** 76104 | **Pieces** 375 | |
| **Year** 2018 | **Minifigures** 4 | |

Thresher can breach a building's walls

Thresher launcher

## ⊙ CORVUS GLAIVE

Corvus Glaive is a fierce warrior who does everything he can to carry out his orders from Thanos. When Corvus is injured during his attack on Vision in Scotland, Proxima Midnight tells the Avengers he died. This lie gives Corvus the element of surprise when he joins the Battle of Wakanda and makes another attempt to steal Vision's Mind Stone. He uses giant Thresher weapons to cause a destructive distraction!

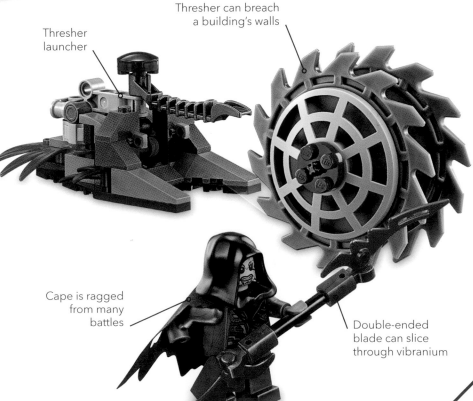

Cape is ragged from many battles

Double-ended blade can slice through vibranium

| Set name | Corvus Glaive Thresher Attack | |
|---|---|---|
| **Number** 76103 | **Pieces** 416 | |
| **Year** 2018 | **Minifigures** 5 | |

# CHITAURI

These fierce, reptilian creatures are Thanos's shock troops. A race of alien warriors, they are naturally fast and very strong. They further enhance their abilities with cybernetic implants and metal armor built directly into their bodies. All Chitauri share a single hive mind, allowing them to act as one, but they can also think for themselves. Their technology is highly advanced and has been salvaged and studied by everyone from S.H.I.E.L.D. to Hydra.

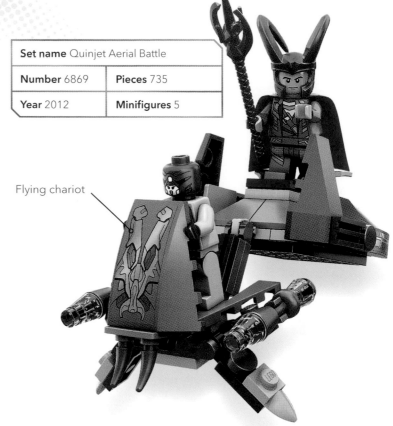

| Set name | Quinjet Aerial Battle | |
|---|---|---|
| Number 6869 | Pieces | 735 |
| Year 2012 | Minifigures | 5 |

Flying chariot

## ▲ ATTACK ON NEW YORK

Asgardian trickster Loki brings the Chitauri to Earth for the first time after making a deal with Thanos. The invading army rides into New York on flying chariots, including one pulling Loki behind it. In this set, they are chased by the Avengers' Quinjet. After a devastating battle, the Avengers defeat the Chitauri by attacking the central command ship that coordinates their hive mind.

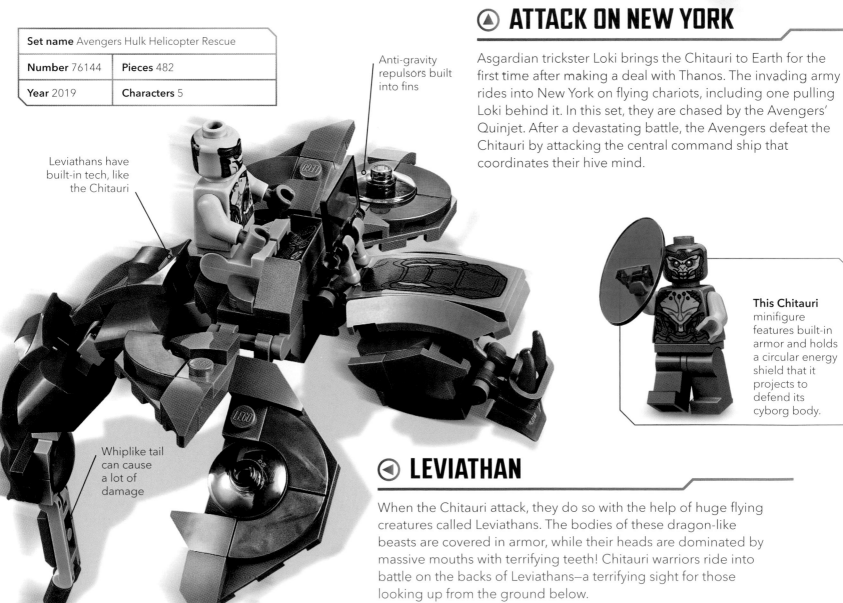

| Set name | Avengers Hulk Helicopter Rescue | |
|---|---|---|
| Number 76144 | Pieces 482 | |
| Year 2019 | Characters 5 | |

Anti-gravity repulsors built into fins

Leviathans have built-in tech, like the Chitauri

Whiplike tail can cause a lot of damage

**This Chitauri** minifigure features built-in armor and holds a circular energy shield that it projects to defend its cyborg body.

## ◀ LEVIATHAN

When the Chitauri attack, they do so with the help of huge flying creatures called Leviathans. The bodies of these dragon-like beasts are covered in armor, while their heads are dominated by massive mouths with terrifying teeth! Chitauri warriors ride into battle on the backs of Leviathans—a terrifying sight for those looking up from the ground below.

# OUTRIDERS

Even more monstrous than the Chitauri, the Outriders are Thanos's relentless foot soldiers. They have no fear, and attack in huge, sprinting packs, easily overwhelming most opponents. Outriders do not carry weapons, relying instead on their immensely powerful limbs, long claws, and fearsome teeth. The Avengers and their allies face hordes of Outriders on the plains of Wakanda, and in the ruins of their compound when Thanos comes in search of Iron Man's Nano Gauntlet.

## ▶ DROPSHIP ATTACK

Thanos sends his Outriders into combat from outer space. His generals launch dagger-shaped dropships, which plunge through the atmosphere and onto the battlefield before spilling out wave upon wave of attackers. Black Widow and Captain America face a fleet of dropships when they team up with Black Panther's army to defend Wakanda. This set has just one LEGO dropship and two Outrider minifigures for Black Widow and Cap to overcome.

Wings open for troops to exit

### BRICK FACTS

Instead of carrying an entire army, the compact LEGO dropship is cleverly designed to seat a pair of Outriders back-to-back.

Black Widow with electro batons

Chitauri pilot

Dropship weapons

| Set name | Outrider Dropship Attack | |
|----------|--------------|-------------|
| Number | 76101 | Pieces 124 |
| Year | 2018 | Minifigures 4 |

Captain America wears Wakandan shields

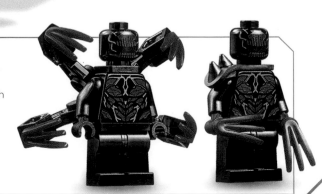

**Outriders have** dark, leathery hides laced with gold armor. Some have as many as six arms, while others have just two.

# ULTRON

Ultron is an artificial intelligence powered by one of the Infinity Stones. Tony Stark and Bruce Banner create Ultron using the Mind Stone, programming him to protect Earth from threats such as the Chitauri. However, Ultron decides that the greatest threat to world peace is humanity itself and sets out to eradicate everyone on the planet! The Avengers look to new members Vision, Wanda Maximoff, and War Machine in order to defeat him.

**Ultron** makes his first body using damaged parts from Tony Stark's team of remote-controlled armors known as the Iron Legion.

**The Ultron Prime** minifigure shows Ultron's second, more powerful, body, which he builds for himself at a Hydra robotics lab.

Flyer is built out of sentry body parts!

Iron Man in Mark 45 armor

Ultron sentries fly like Iron Man

## ▶ ULTRON SENTRIES

Ultron builds an army of robot sentries in his own image and unleashes them on the Avengers in Sokovia. When the Avengers foil his plan to lift an entire city into the sky and then drop it like a bomb, he flees the scene by uploading his mind into his last remaining sentry. This set comes with three Ultron sentries and Iron Man, who chases them through the air.

| Set name | Iron Man Vs. Ultron | |
|---|---|---|
| Number | 76029 | Pieces 92 |
| Year | 2015 | Minifigures 4 |

# OTHER POWERFUL BEINGS

The Multiverse is home to many beings, some of whom have powers most Super Heroes can only dream of! The once peaceful Gorr acquires Asgardian levels of strength and a terrible thirst for vengeance when he is corrupted by an ancient sword. The being known as The Watcher, meanwhile, is just about the most powerful force in any reality, but he has sworn not to use his abilities to influence the destiny of mortals.

**The Watcher** is a cosmic being who dwells in the Observational Plane, where he can view every "What if..." scenario in The Multiverse! His minifigure wears The Watcher uniform with golden chestplate.

**Gorr's head piece** features his tattoo markings, and he holds his Necrosword. The ancient sword allows Gorr to summon shadow monsters, as well as giving him devastating strength.

Helmet supports MODOK's heavy head

## ◀ MODOK

When AIM scientists transform one of their own technicians to give him the world's biggest brain, they create a power-hungry genius with psychic powers! Too weak to carry his huge head by himself, MODOK relies on a hover chair to move around, and he wears a headband that focuses his vast amounts of mental energy into highly destructive blasts.

Rockets power MODOK's flying chair

| Set name | Avengers: Hulk Lab Smash | | |
|---|---|---|---|
| **Number** 76018 | | **Pieces** 398 | |
| **Year** 2014 | | **Characters** 5 | |

### BRICK FACTS

While the MODOK in Hulk Lab Smash uses mostly minifigure parts, the version in Avengers Helicarrier (set 76153) is entirely brick-built.

**Hyperion** is a powerful alien who presents himself as a Super Hero but wants to "save" planets by ruling them like a tyrant.

# HUMAN VILLAINS

Not every villain faced by the Avengers has super-powers. Some are just very clever, very determined, or equipped with very advanced technology! Obadiah Stane, Ivan Vanko, and Justin Hammer are all talented engineers whose loathing for Tony Stark causes them to redirect their skills to channel revenge and destruction. Ulysses Klaue, meanwhile, is a wily crook with a grudge against Black Panther, and a powerful Wakandan mining tool built into his body as a weapon!

| Set name Iron Man: Iron Monger Mayhem | |
|---|---|
| Number 76190 | Pieces 479 |
| Year 2021 | Minifigures 3 |

Wrist-mounted cannon

Arc Reactor stolen from Tony Stark

Exposed pistons power both huge legs

Palm repulsors enable flight

**Obadiah Stane** helped Tony Stark's father set up Stark Industries. His minifigure might look charming in a sleek business suit, but Stane loathes Tony for changing the company's direction.

## ▶ IRON MONGER

Businessman Obadiah Stane believes he should be in charge of Stark Industries, and makes several attempts to defeat Tony Stark. He copies the original Iron Man armor to make his Iron Monger suit, and steals Stark's Arc Reactor to power it. He very nearly defeats Iron Man in battle, but Pepper Potts comes to the rescue.

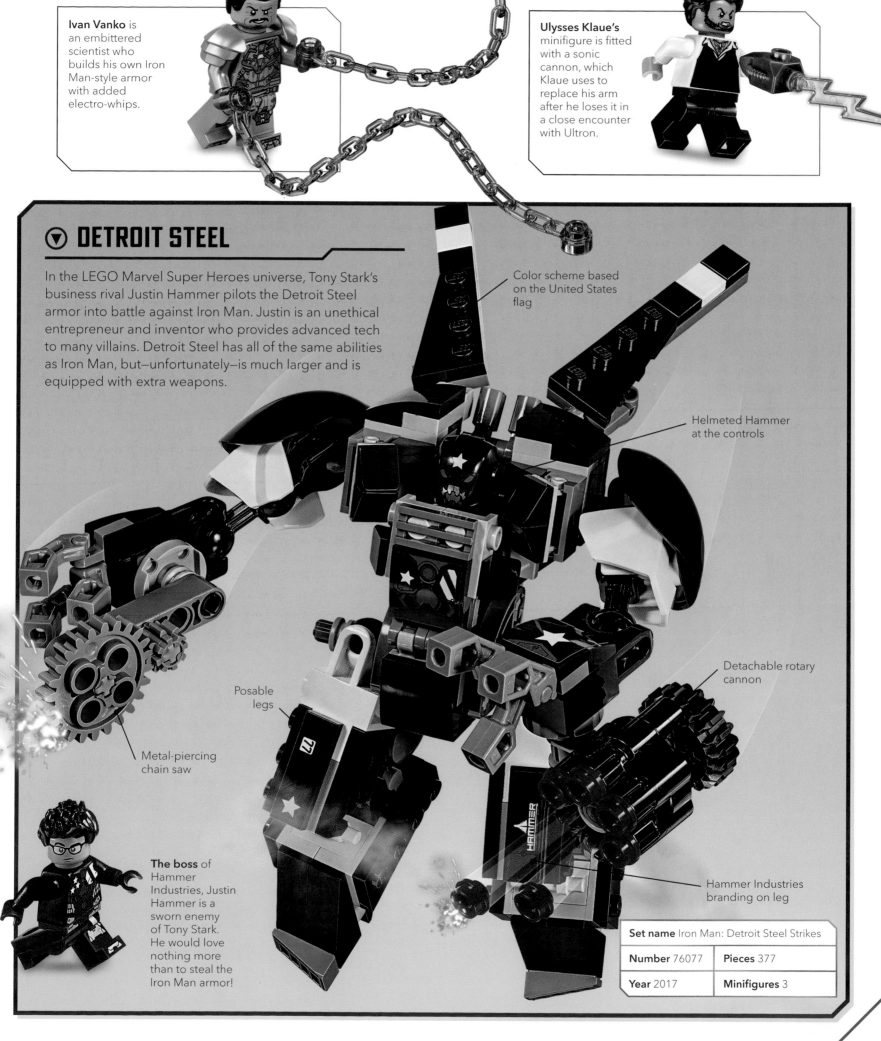

**Ivan Vanko** is an embittered scientist who builds his own Iron Man-style armor with added electro-whips.

**Ulysses Klaue's** minifigure is fitted with a sonic cannon, which Klaue uses to replace his arm after he loses it in a close encounter with Ultron.

# DETROIT STEEL

In the LEGO Marvel Super Heroes universe, Tony Stark's business rival Justin Hammer pilots the Detroit Steel armor into battle against Iron Man. Justin is an unethical entrepreneur and inventor who provides advanced tech to many villains. Detroit Steel has all of the same abilities as Iron Man, but—unfortunately—is much larger and is equipped with extra weapons.

Color scheme based on the United States flag

Helmeted Hammer at the controls

Detachable rotary cannon

Posable legs

Metal-piercing chain saw

Hammer Industries branding on leg

**The boss** of Hammer Industries, Justin Hammer is a sworn enemy of Tony Stark. He would love nothing more than to steal the Iron Man armor!

| Set name | Iron Man: Detroit Steel Strikes | |
|---|---|---|
| Number | 76077 | Pieces | 377 |
| Year | 2017 | Minifigures | 3 |

# SAKAAR

Most of the galaxy thinks of the planet Sakaar as a remote wasteland, but its ruler, the Grandmaster, treats it like a giant playground. For all his seeming good humor, the Grandmaster has a darker side. He forces some people to fight for his amusement, and others to live as scavengers. Few beings travel to Sakaar willingly, and those who come to be there try not to stay for long if they have any choice in the matter. Among those who find themselves stuck on the planet are Hulk, Thor, Loki, and the self-exiled Asgardian Valkyrie.

**The flamboyant Grandmaster** rules Sakaar from a grand palace. His minifigure is dressed in shiny gold robes and has a blue chin stripe.

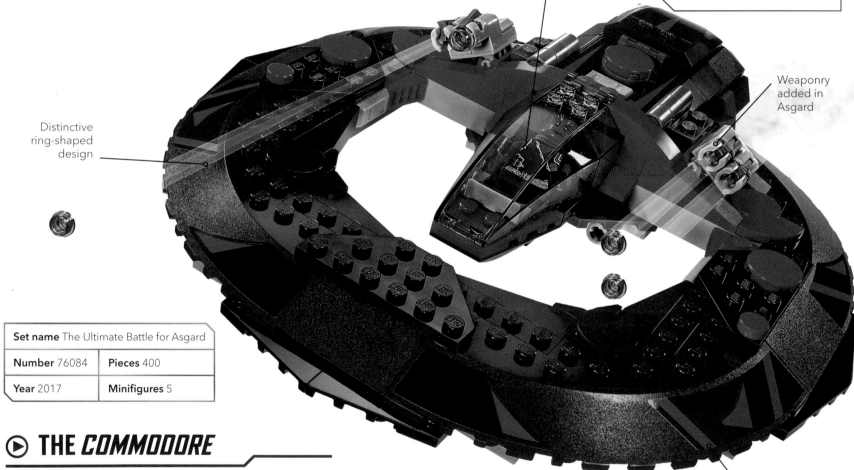

Valkyrie is a skilled starship pilot

Weaponry added in Asgard

Distinctive ring-shaped design

Bright colors reflect the Grandmaster's gaudy style

| Set name | The Ultimate Battle for Asgard | |
|---|---|---|
| Number 76084 | Pieces 400 | |
| Year 2017 | Minifigures 5 | |

## ▶ THE *COMMODORE*

The *Commodore* is one of the Grandmaster's favorite party ships, until it is stolen by Thor to escape from Sakaar. Valkyrie and Bruce Banner join him on board, and the trio pilot the vessel through a wormhole to Asgard and equip it for combat against Hela and her Berserker warriors.

**Korg,** a rocky Kronan, lives on Sakaar as one of the Grandmaster's gladiators until Valkyrie helps him lead a revolt. His minifigure appears in Endgame Battle (set 40525).

**Miek is a member** of an insectoid species. Her minifigure's exoskeleton is built from bricks and blades, topped with a purple head, and comes in Endgame Battle (set 40525).

# TALOKAN

Just like Wakanda, Talokan is a kingdom shaped by vibranium. Unlike Wakanda, Talokan is hidden deep under the sea! It was founded when a group of people ingested a vibranium-enhanced medicine that turned them into water-breathers. They made their new home in the Atlantic Ocean and built an advanced civilization using the vibranium deposits located there. Talokan's existence remains a secret for centuries—until scientists start searching the seas for precious vibranium.

| Set name | King Namor's Throne Room | |
| --- | --- | --- |
| Number 76213 | | Pieces 355 |
| Year 2022 | | Minifigures 3 |

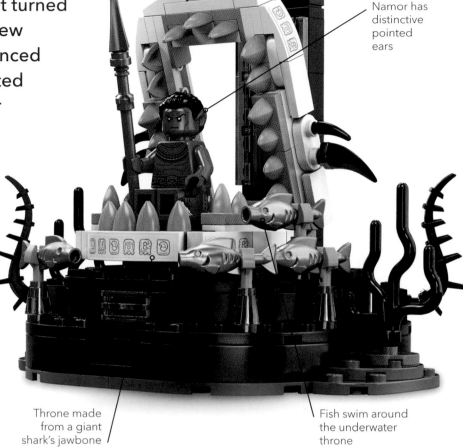

Namor has distinctive pointed ears

Throne made from a giant shark's jawbone

Fish swim around the underwater throne

## ▶ NAMOR

Talokan is ruled by Namor, the first Talokanil to be born underwater. Unlike the rest of his people, Namor can breathe in air as well as water and can fly, thanks to wings on his feet! He is deeply suspicious of outsiders and is willing to go to war to protect his kingdom.

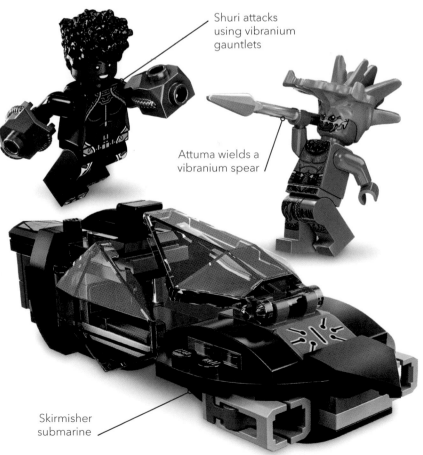

Shuri attacks using vibranium gauntlets

Attuma wields a vibranium spear

Skirmisher submarine

## ◀ UNDERWATER ATTACK

Fiercely protective of Talokan's vibranium, Namor and his people clash with Wakanda, who refuse to ally with them for war. Shuri, the new Black Panther, faces off against Attuma, one of Namor's advisors and greatest warriors. Wakandan underwater vehicles head into battle, including a skirmisher submarine, which shoots stud missiles against the Talokan guards.

### BRICK FACTS

The compact Wakandan submarine fits a minifigure pilot lying in an almost horizontal position. Transparent blue bricks show the sub's vibranium elements.

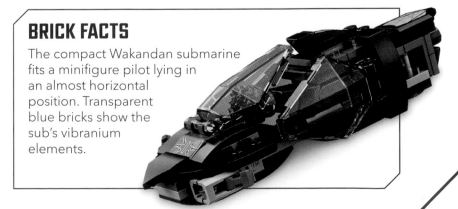

# Chapter 3:
# GUARDIANS OF THE GALAXY AND OTHER TEAMS

# STAR-LORD

Abducted from Earth as a young boy, Peter Quill is raised by an alien named Yondu. Quill grows up as a member of Yondu's outlaw clan, the Ravagers, and becomes a carefree crook who goes by the name of Star-Lord. Quill eventually finds himself in prison, where he teams up with other inmates—Gamora, Rocket, Groot, and Drax—to escape. Adventure leads this ragtag crew to risk their own lives to save a planet, and they became a team—the Guardians of the Galaxy! Star-Lord thinks of himself as their leader.

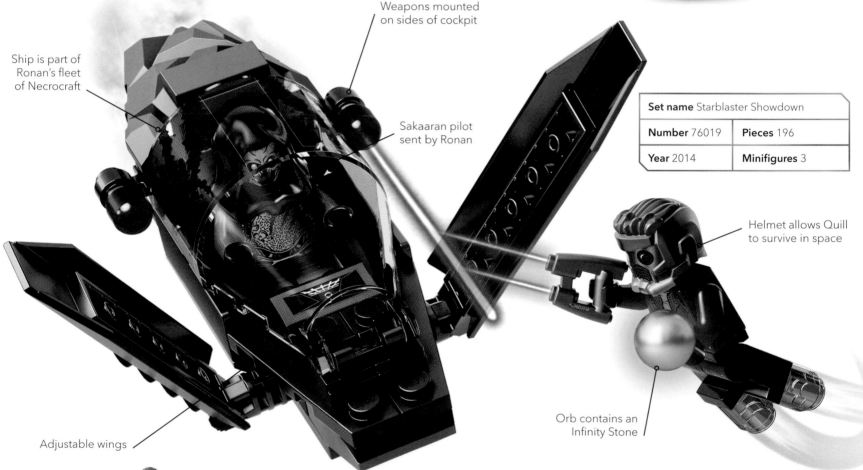

Weapons mounted on sides of cockpit

Ship is part of Ronan's fleet of Necrocraft

Sakaaran pilot sent by Ronan

Helmet allows Quill to survive in space

Orb contains an Infinity Stone

Adjustable wings

| Set name | Starblaster Showdown | |
|---|---|---|
| Number 76019 | Pieces 196 | |
| Year 2014 | Minifigures 3 | |

### QUILL VS. RONAN

The first time Peter faces Ronan the Accuser, in The Milano Space Ship Rescue (set 76021), he blasts him with a large Hadron Enforcer space blaster—with no effect!

## ⏵ RACE FOR THE STONE

Star-Lord's journey to becoming a hero begins when he unwittingly takes possession of an immensely powerful Infinity Stone. The Kree warlord Ronan the Accuser wants the stone so he can attack the planet Xandar, and sends his Sakaaran army to get it. Fortunately, Star-Lord is equipped for space battles, with his personalized helmet, jet boots, and trusty quadblaster.

# TEAMWORK

After their first victory as the Guardians of the Galaxy, the group decides to stay together. Working as a team has its rocky moments, but each of the Guardians learns from their teammates. Having started out as enemies, Quill and Gamora even end up falling in love! They manage to have fun on their missions—even when they're battling terrifying enemies!

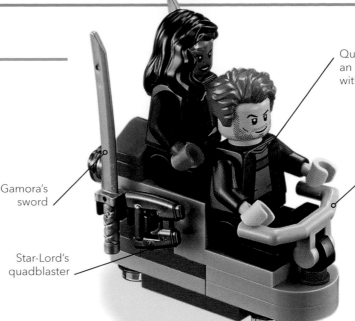

Quill heads off on an adventure with Gamora

Space scooter disembarks from the Guardians' ship

Gamora's sword

Star-Lord's quadblaster

| Set name | Thanos: Ultimate Battle | |
|---|---|---|
| Number | 76107 | Pieces 674 |
| Year | 2018 | Characters 4 |

## GOD OR LORD?

When Thor makes himself at home on the Guardians' ship in set 76193, Quill worries he might take over as the team's leader! But Thor is interested only in creating a new weapon and eating LEGO® donuts.

## BRICK FACTS

The Guardians' *Milano* ship in set 76081 comes with one of Quill's most treasured possessions: an "Awesome Mix" tape of classic rock songs made for him by his mom.

# LASER DRILL ATTACK

Growing up, Quill looked up to Yondu as a father figure. While the leader of the Ravagers genuinely cared for Quill, he never showed him any kindness, and the two became fierce rivals. Years later, however, Star-Lord and Yondu team up against a greater threat. Yondu's Laser Drill spaceship carries him and Star-Lord into battle against a power-crazed Celestial being, who just might be Star-Lord's biological dad…

Red uniform of Yondu's clan, the Ravagers

Ravagers symbol obscures original decals

**The red spike** on top of Yondu's head piece isn't his hair—it's the interface for a fearsome arrow weapon he controls by whistling!

Laser Drill ship is designed for mining

| Set name | Ayesha's Revenge | |
|---|---|---|
| Number | 76080 | Pieces 323 |
| Year | 2017 | Characters 4 |

# THE MILANO

The Guardians' first headquarters is this M-ship named the *Milano*, originally part of a fleet belonging to Yondu's clan, the Ravagers. When Star-Lord was still a member of the Ravagers, he made the *Milano* his home, decking it out with personal touches such as a tape deck to play his "Awesome Mix Vol. I." When he quits Yondu's clan, he takes the vessel with him and uses it to escape from prison with his new gang, who will later become the Guardians of the Galaxy.

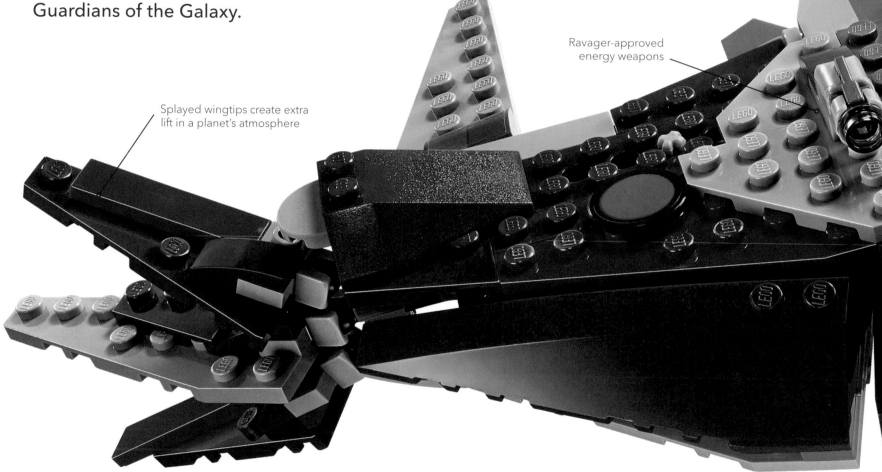

Splayed wingtips create extra lift in a planet's atmosphere

Ravager-approved energy weapons

### ALL ABOARD!

M-ships are designed for a crew of four. The *Milano*'s cockpit has stations for piloting, navigation, communications, and weapons control—plus enough space to squeeze in the Baby Groot LEGO figure as well.

## ⊙ DOUBLE DESTRUCTION

The *Milano* doesn't survive the Guardians' battle to save the planet Xandar, but the local authorities rebuild the ship to show their thanks. The Guardians travel on the new *Milano* to collect Gamora's sister, Nebula, from the planet Sovereign, but it, too, is damaged beyond repair when an attack by Sovereign's massive fleet causes it to crash-land. This set features the rebuilt version of the *Milano* that flies to Sovereign. It is equipped with stud shooters and has a bomb-dropping function to help the Guardians during the battle.

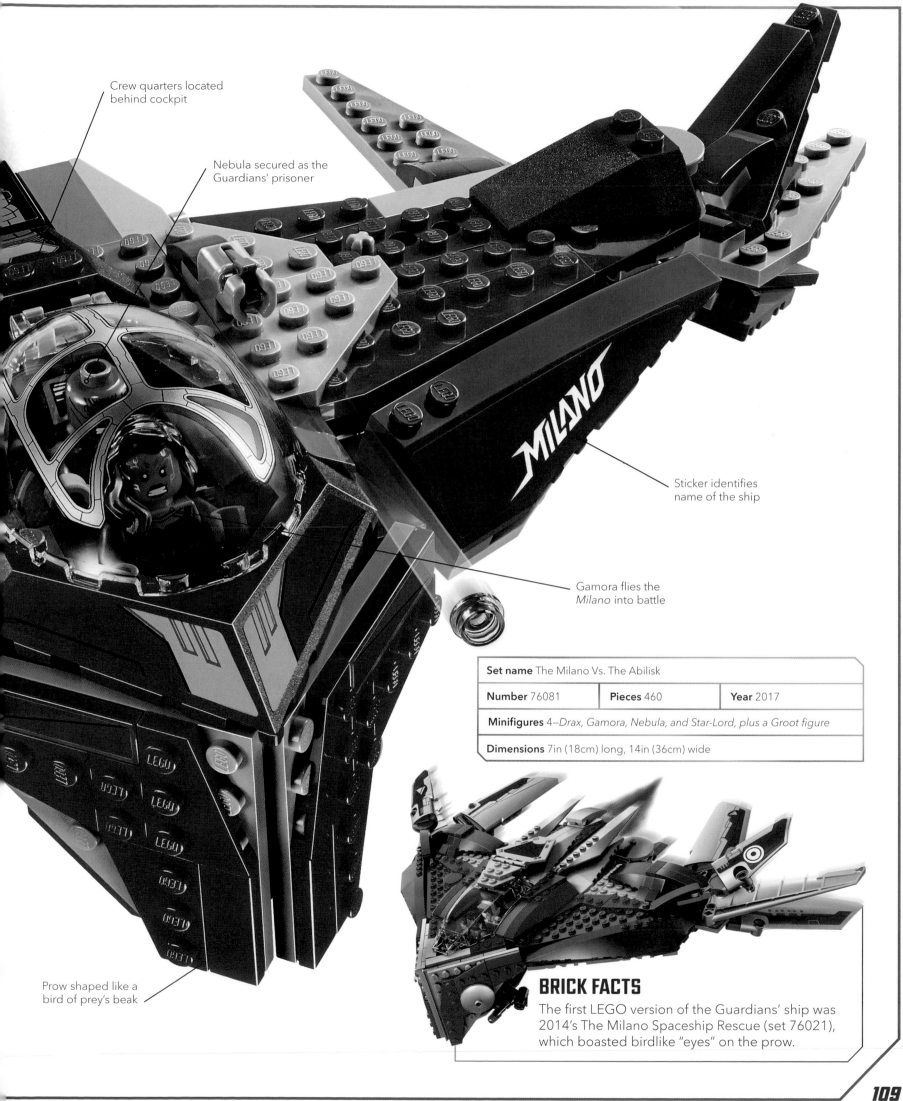

Crew quarters located
behind cockpit

Nebula secured as the
Guardians' prisoner

Sticker identifies
name of the ship

Gamora flies the
*Milano* into battle

| Set name | The Milano Vs. The Abilisk | | |
|---|---|---|---|
| **Number** 76081 | | **Pieces** 460 | **Year** 2017 |
| **Minifigures** 4–Drax, Gamora, Nebula, and Star-Lord, plus a Groot figure | | | |
| **Dimensions** 7in (18cm) long, 14in (36cm) wide | | | |

Prow shaped like a
bird of prey's beak

## BRICK FACTS

The first LEGO version of the Guardians' ship was
2014's The Milano Spaceship Rescue (set 76021),
which boasted birdlike "eyes" on the prow.

# ROCKET

Rocket is a unique creature—the result of illegal experiments. He is super smart and strong but also bitter and distrustful because of what was done to him. Along with his best friend, Groot, Rocket lives as a thief and bounty hunter until he tries to collect the bounty on Peter Quill. The resulting battle brings Rocket and Quill together—first in jail, and then as Guardians of the Galaxy!

Rotating side panels control movement

Cramped cockpit

Mechanical mining claws

## ◀ POD ESCAPE

The Guardians' first mission as a team takes them to a lawless mining outpost named Knowhere. When they are attacked, Rocket calls on his piloting skills—and all his nerve—to fly a tough but unarmed mining pod past the enemy fleet and out into space. The LEGO pod's gripping arms can hold on to the mysterious Orb, which is the cause of all the trouble.

| Set name | Knowhere Escape Mission | |
|---|---|---|
| Number 76020 | Pieces 433 | |
| Year 2014 | Characters 3 | |

## ▶ RAVAGER AMBUSH

Rocket is a quick thinker and an excellent problem solver. Stranded on the planet Berhert with Groot and Nebula, he rigs up an array of traps in the trees to protect against attackers. When the Ravagers arrive to capture the team, Rocket's tricks stop them in their tracks.

**Rocket's minifigure** wears a Time Suit when he joins the Avengers on a mission to save his fellow Guardians from Thanos.

Laser cannon with targeting scope

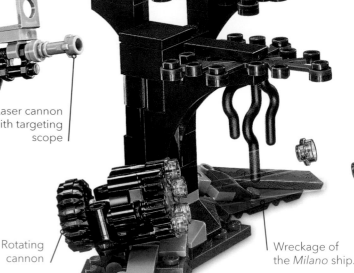

| Set name | Ravager Attack | |
|---|---|---|
| Number 76079 | Pieces 197 | |
| Year 2017 | Characters 3 | |

Rotating cannon

Wreckage of the *Milano* ship.

# GROOT

The giant, treelike Groot becomes a Guardian of the Galaxy through his partnership with Rocket. He is brave in battle and grows himself into a leafy cocoon to protect his teammates from a devastating crash. Only a small sprig from Groot's body survives, and it slowly grows into a whole new being under Rocket's care. Baby Groot has since become a sulky teen, but he remains a valuable member of the Guardians.

**When Baby Groot** and Rocket joined the Ravagers for a short time, the clan made a mini uniform to fit the tiny tree!

## ⊽ NIDAVELLIR FORGE

Groot and Rocket travel with Thor to the cosmic forge of Nidavellir, hoping to create a new weapon for Thor to use against Thanos. Weakened by the vast energies of the forge, Thor is unable to complete his mighty Stormbreaker axe, until Groot gives his left arm to use as the weapon's handle.

**BRICK FACTS**

The giant Groot in 2014's Knowhere Escape Mission (set 76020) is designed so Rocket can stand on his brick-built biceps!

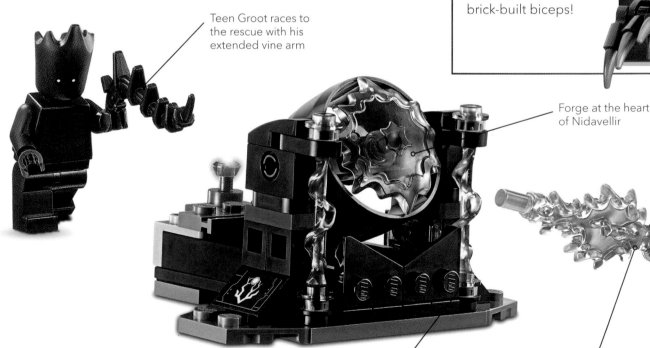

Teen Groot races to the rescue with his extended vine arm

Forge at the heart of Nidavellir

Cosmic energy

Thor channels the energy of a neutron star to ignite the forge

| Set name Thor's Weapon Quest | |
|---|---|
| **Number** 76102 | **Pieces** 223 |
| **Year** 2018 | **Characters** 3 |

# GAMORA

Gamora grows up as one of Thanos's children, an army of youngsters collected and trained by Thanos. Gamora is endlessly pitted against her adopted sister, Nebula. Both become utterly ruthless warriors, but Gamora has always been Thanos's favorite. However, Gamora longs to escape from Thanos's influence, and she gets the chance when she's sent to steal an Infinity Stone from Peter Quill. She ends up joining forces with Quill as one of the Guardians of the Galaxy and later convinces Nebula to join the fight against Thanos as well.

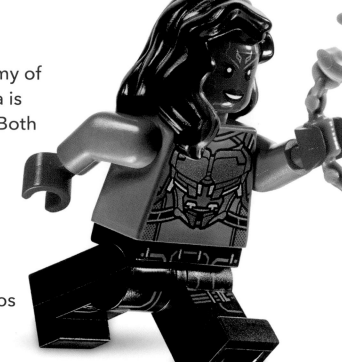

"Big fig" represents an illusion of Thanos created by the Reality Stone

Gamora's sword

"Big figs" are almost twice as tall as regular minifigures

## ◉ FATHER VS. DAUGHTER

Gamora comes up against Thanos again as he continues his hunt for the Infinity Stones. She attacks, and it seems as though she has defeated him, only for her to realize she is battling an illusion! The LEGO "big fig" Thanos in this set is no illusion, however, and it comes with an oversize sword and the Infinity Gauntlet, containing one red Infinity Stone.

| Set name Thanos: Ultimate Battle | |
|---|---|
| **Number** 76107 | **Pieces** 674 |
| **Year** 2018 | **Characters** 4 |

## SKY SKILLS

Gamora is a talented pilot as well as a warrior. She can fly anything, from a small mining pod to the speedy *Milano*. The happy expression on her dual-sided head piece shows just how much she enjoys flying!

**Nebula is Gamora's** cybernetic sister who stays loyal to Thanos for a very long time. Her minifigure shows her patched-up cyborg body with details on her head piece and different color arms.

## SISTERS AVENGED

When Gamora saves Nebula's life, it convinces her to finally abandon Thanos. The reformed Nebula joins the Avengers and fights against Thanos in the final battle.

# DRAX

Drax is an angry criminal locked up in jail, until he meets the other Guardians. He lost his home and family to the forces of Thanos and his Kree soldier, Ronan the Accuser, so Drax's sole focus in life is revenge. However, the Guardians become his new family, and Drax realizes he has more to offer than just revenge. He helps his new team save another world from Ronan and finally finds some peace. A Guardian of the Galaxy ever since, Drax's immense strength helps them on many missions, and he also fights alongside the Avengers in their final showdown with Thanos.

Drax has tattoos all over his body

Abilisk's mouth opens and closes to swallow Drax

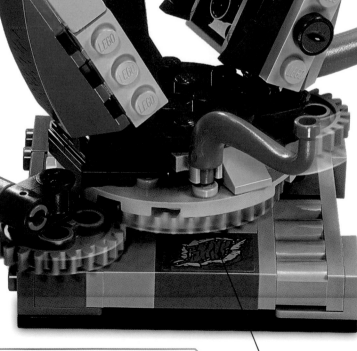

Abilisks also use their tentacles to fly!

## ◉ ABILISK ATTACK

Drax is a fearless warrior with little respect for his own safety. When the Guardians battle a giant Abilisk monster, he lets the creature eat him so he can fight it from the inside! It takes the whole team to defeat the Abilisk, but Drax deserves the credit when he emerges from its gory guts! While Drax's minifigure cannnot fit inside the LEGO Abilisk's mouth completely, he can be clamped in its sharp teeth.

**Mantis is an insectoid** empath who joins the Guardians and becomes Drax's best friend. Her antennae are part of the hair piece, which is exclusive to Mantis minifigures.

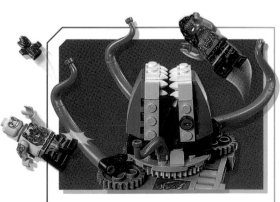

## BRICK FACTS

The LEGO Abilisk in this set is built with a mechanism that allows the tentacles to flail around when the creature's head is turned!

Sticker allows the rest of the monster's pink body to be glimpsed through this rubble

| Set name | The Milano Vs. The Abilisk | |
|---|---|---|
| Number 76081 | | Pieces 460 |
| Year 2017 | | Characters 5 |

# THE GUARDIANS' SECOND SHIP

After abandoning the shipwrecked *Milano* on the planet Berhart, the Guardians upgrade to this more advanced M-class vessel. It is in this ship that they first encounter Thor, who tells the team about Thanos's plans to wipe out half of the universe. The Guardians cannot stop Thanos when they face him on the planet Titan, but when the Avengers take the ship to Earth, it becomes a vital tool in their mission to rewrite history for the better.

## ▼ SHRINKING SHIP

Star-Lord thinks of all the Guardians' ships as his own, but this one has soared under the command of many others. Hawkeye and Black Widow fly the ship—after it is shrunk down, sent through a quantum tunnel, and returned to its original size—during the mission to undo Thanos's seemingly final triumph.

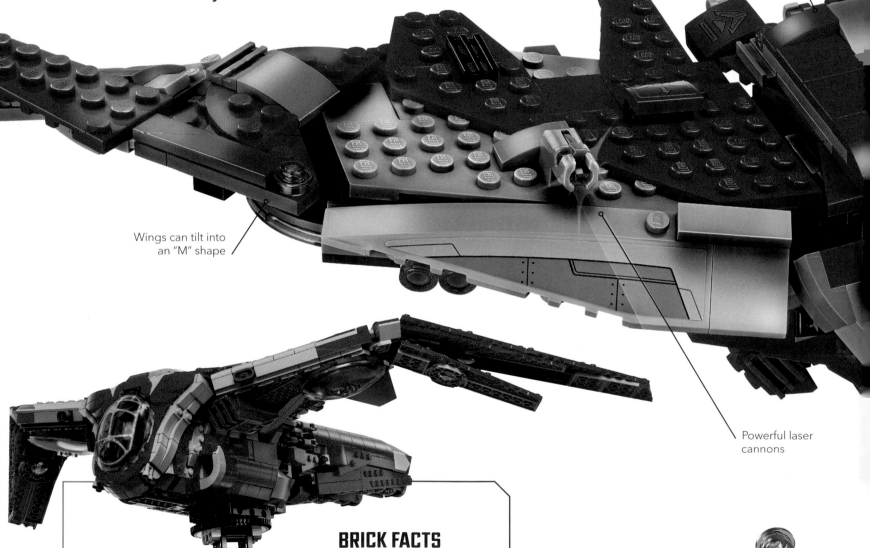

Docking area for rear pod

Wings can tilt into an "M" shape

Powerful laser cannons

## BRICK FACTS

An even larger, 1,901-piece version of The Guardians' Ship (set 76193) was released in 2021, complete with an adjustable display stand.

| Set name | Thanos: Ultimate Battle | |
|---|---|---|
| **Number** 76107 | **Pieces** 674 | |
| **Year** 2018 | **Characters** 4 | |

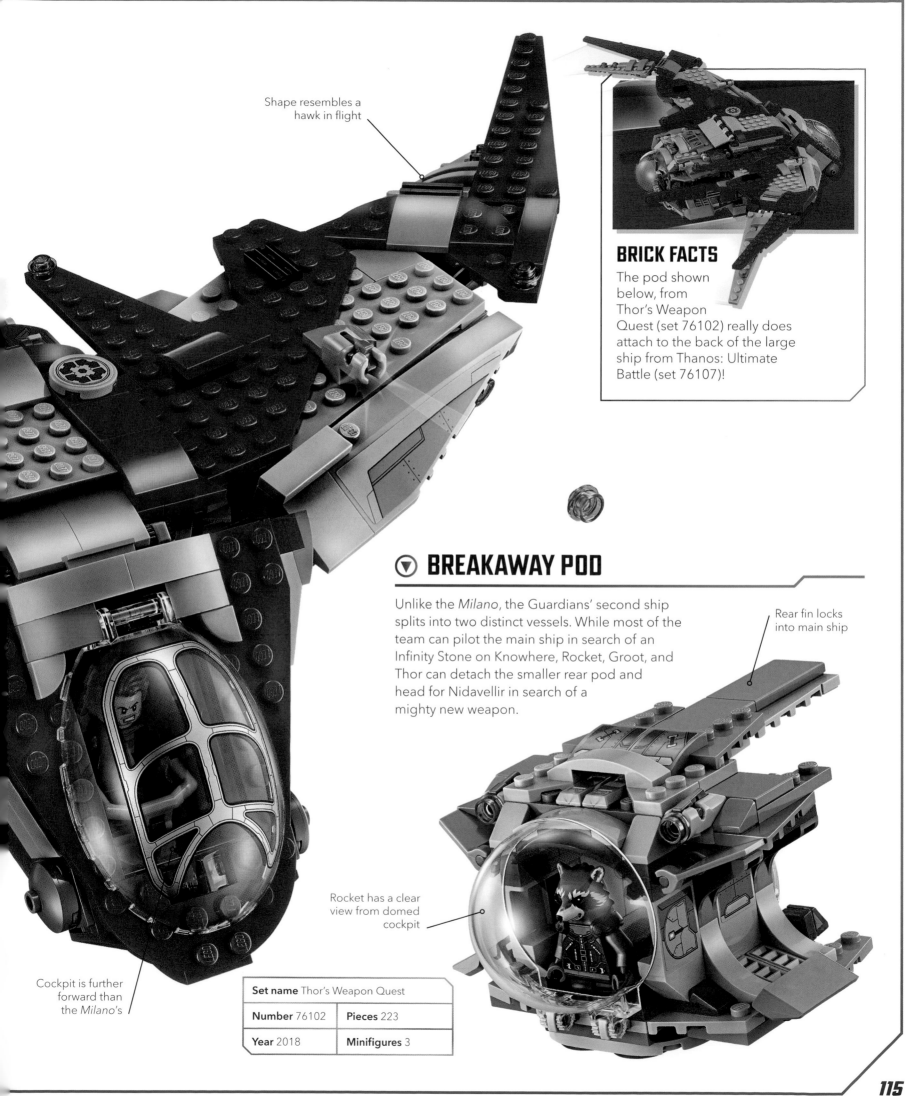

Shape resembles a hawk in flight

## BRICK FACTS

The pod shown below, from Thor's Weapon Quest (set 76102) really does attach to the back of the large ship from Thanos: Ultimate Battle (set 76107)!

## ▼ BREAKAWAY POD

Unlike the *Milano*, the Guardians' second ship splits into two distinct vessels. While most of the team can pilot the main ship in search of an Infinity Stone on Knowhere, Rocket, Groot, and Thor can detach the smaller rear pod and head for Nidavellir in search of a mighty new weapon.

Rear fin locks into main ship

Rocket has a clear view from domed cockpit

Cockpit is further forward than the *Milano*'s

| Set name | Thor's Weapon Quest | |
|---|---|---|
| **Number** 76102 | **Pieces** 223 | |
| **Year** 2018 | **Minifigures** 3 | |

# ENEMIES OF THE GUARDIANS

Though they would love an easy life, nothing is ever simple for the Guardians of the Galaxy. Some of their foes, such as the Nova Corps, go on to become invaluable friends, while partners such as Ayesha and the Sovereign become implacable enemies. In fact, even the Guardians themselves have complicated origins. Gamora was an ally of Ronan the Accuser before managing to escape his influence, and Star-Lord was once in the same clan as Taserface, back when he was part of the Ravagers!

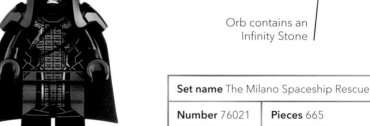

Sakaaran-controlled Necrocraft

## ▶ CLASH WITH RONAN

A Kree military leader turned warlord, Ronan the Accuser goes rogue when his people choose a path of peace. He raises a personal army of Sakaarans and uses one of the Infinity Stones to attack the planet Xandar in his Necrocraft starship. But Ronan is foiled by a ragtag band of convicts that he sarcastically names the "Guardians of the Galaxy."

Orb contains an Infinity Stone

Ronan's chain-mail armor dates from his time as leader of the Accusers, the Kree Empire's most fearsome warriors.

| Set name | The Milano Spaceship Rescue | |
|---|---|---|
| **Number** 76021 | | **Pieces** 665 |
| **Year** 2014 | | **Minifigures** 5 |

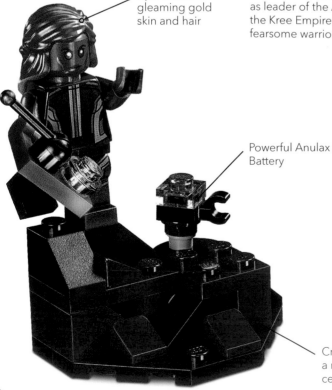

Ayesha has gleaming gold skin and hair

Powerful Anulax Battery

## ◀ AYESHA

Ayesha is the Golden High Priestess of the people known as the Sovereign. She hires the Guardians to save her planet's power source from a hungry space monster, but when Rocket steals precious Anulax Batteries, Ayesha swears revenge! She sends her flying droids after the Guardians, resulting in a deadly space battle.

Craft is piloted from a mission control center

Ayesha's Golden Drone has adjustable arms and two stud shooters

# FACING TASERFACE

The Guardians face off against this poorly named pirate when he seizes control of Star-Lord's old clan, the Ravagers. Taserface takes Yondu, Groot, and Rocket prisoner, but they escape and wreck his ship in the process. Rocket also finds time to annoy Taserface with lots of jokes about his name, which the villain gave to himself to sound scary!

Ravagers symbol

Turbine engine

**Taserface's minifigure**
wears the dark red uniform of Yondu's Ravagers clan. The Ravagers' spiky symbol is just visible behind his beard!

Typical Ravager M-ship

Missile launcher

| Set name Ravager Attack | |
| --- | --- |
| **Number** 76079 | **Pieces** 197 |
| **Year** 2017 | **Characters** 3 |

Fins can close up for speed or fan out for defense

| Set name Starblaster Showdown | |
| --- | --- |
| **Number** 76019 | **Pieces** 196 |
| **Year** 2014 | **Minifigures** 3 |

# NOVA CORPS

Star-Lord was a thorn in the side of this interplanetary police force before he became a Guardian. In fact, it was the Nova Corps arrest of Peter, Gamora, Groot, and Rocket that first brought the team together! The Guardians and Nova Corps eventually team up to defend the Corps' base planet, Xandar, from Ronan the Accuser. A fleet of ships called Star Blasters take to the skies to protect their planet. In this set, the Star Blaster takes on a Sakaaran Necrocraft, while Star-Lord joins the battle using his boot thrusters.

Cockpit for a single Nova Corps pilot

**Nova Corps officers**
wear helmets with a red starburst symbol and armor with three gold lights representing Xandar's trio of suns.

Star Blaster in the Nova Corps colors of blue and gold

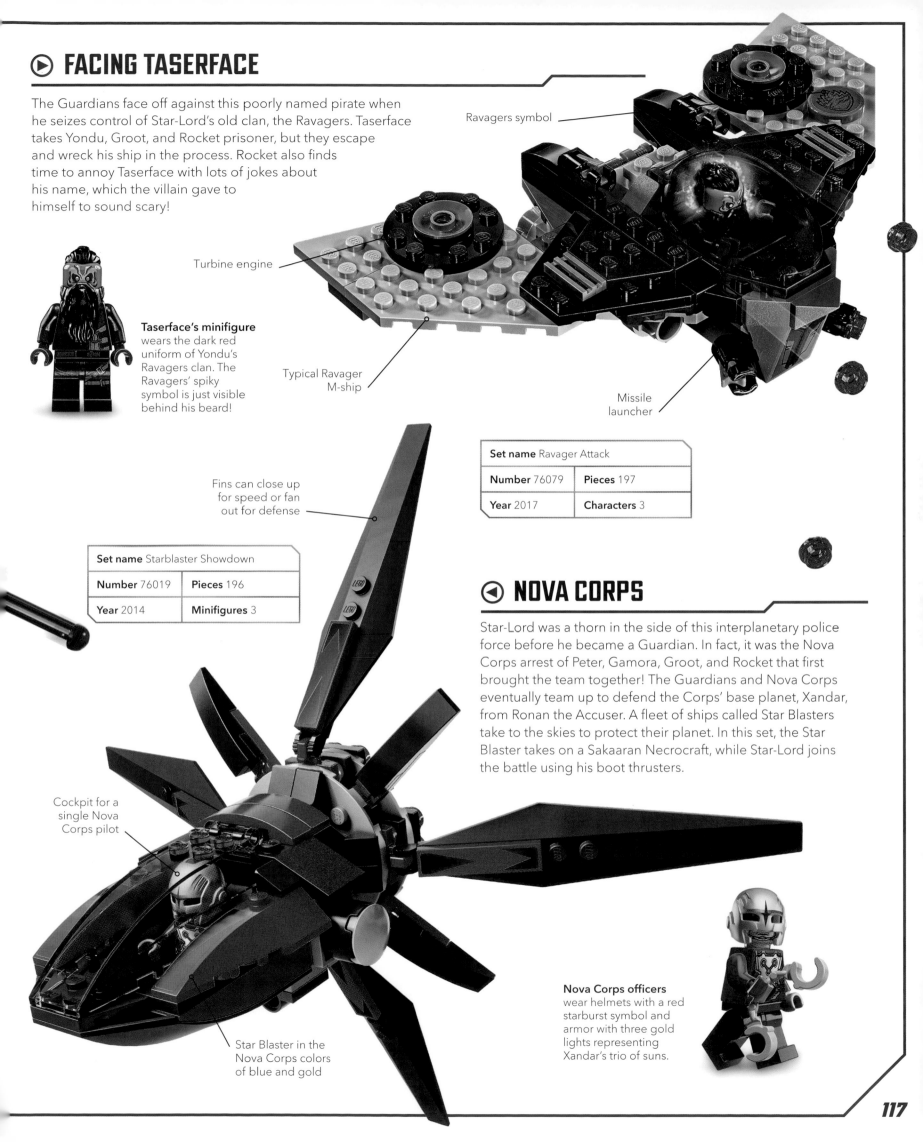

# THE GUARDIANS' NEW SHIP

The Guardians' first two ships both had a hawklike shape, but their latest is something different altogether! Its four engines attach to the main hull on two vast rings, and when it lands, the front opens up, allowing the team to make a dramatic entrance down a mouthlike ramp. The new ship is also equipped with advanced energy weapons to defend against attack and a cloaking device that can turn it invisible at the flick of a switch.

## ▶ OUT OF KNOWHERE

The Guardians of the Galaxy get their new ship when they set up a permanent base at Knowhere, docking it alongside their second ship. Drax and Mantis travel in the new ship to Earth, in search of the perfect Christmas present for Peter Quill, before the whole team comes on board and takes the ship on a far more dangerous mission. Three minifigures can fit into the ship's spacious cockpit, while another can hide in a secret compartment.

Adam Warlock attacks

Hatch opens to reveal hidden weapons store

| Set name The New Guardians' Ship | |
|---|---|
| **Number** 76255 | **Pieces** 1,108 |
| **Year** 2023 | **Minifigures** 5 |

### BRICK FACTS

The New Guardians' Ship set comes with a sleek display stand to really show off its three-minifigure cockpit, opening ramp, and two breakaway support craft!

**Adam Warlock** was created by the Sovereign to take down the Guardians. He is immensely strong, but his mind is very young.

**Nebula** and the rest of the Guardians show off a cool new look in their cool new ship, with stylish matching uniforms.

Quill and Nebula in the cockpit

## ROCKET'S SHIP

When Rocket was a young, ordinary raccoon, a cruel scientist known as The High Evolutionary carried out experiments that ended up making Rocket super-intelligent. The High Evolutionary wants Rocket to be part of a new "perfect" society, but instead the tiny creature uses his new-found brilliance to steal this small, yellow ship and make a spectacular getaway.

Entry/exit ramp can open and close

Missile launcher

Engines rotate for takeoff and landing

Baby Rocket

**Baby Rocket** is a unique figure featuring special face printing on a LEGO raccoon element originally created for the LEGO® Friends theme.

| Set name Baby Rocket's Ship | |
|---|---|
| **Number** 76254 | **Pieces** 330 |
| **Year** 2023 | **Minifigures** 1 |

# ETERNALS

More than 7,000 years ago, a team of ten Eternals came to Earth to protect it from alien creatures called Deviants. The Eternals are human in appearance, though they don't appear to age. Today, they still live on Earth, keeping watch in case the Deviant threat should return. The team members do not always agree about the best way to co-exist with human beings, but they have all sworn loyalty to their Celestial leader, Arishem.

## ⊙ THE *DOMO*

The Eternals arrive on Earth on a huge, wedge-shaped starship called the *Domo*. They hide it underground and use it as their base for thousands of years. By the 21st century, only one team member—Makkari—lives on board, but the *Domo* flies once more when a new threat reunites the team. The *Domo* opens up to accommodate the Eternals minifigures in the cockpit, grand chamber, and armory. There's even a coffee machine at the ready!

| Set name | Rise of the Domo | |
|---|---|---|
| Number 76156 | | Pieces 1,040 |
| Year 2021 | | Minifigures 6 |

Geometric patterns generate Celestial energy to power the ship

## ⊙ MEET THE TEAM

**Ajak**
The leader of the group is also its telepathic link to the Celestials. She can heal any injury in seconds.

**Sersi**
Sersi can transform matter with a touch, but hides her powers to live as a museum curator in 21st-century London.

**Ikaris**
Ikaris can fly and fire cosmic energy beams from his eyes. His romance with Sersi lasts for thousands of years.

**Kingo**
Kingo's ability to project cosmic energy from his hands is matched only by his magnetism as a Bollywood film star!

**Sprite**
An old soul in a never-aging child's body, Sprite can create lifelike illusions, real enough to fool even other Eternals.

**Phastos**
The team's tech expert has been responsible for many of Earth's scientific innovations since around 5,000 BCE—in secret, of course!

**Makkari**
Makkari moves so fast she can create sonic booms! She is personally unaffected by these noisy blasts because she is deaf.

**Druig**
Druig uses his strong will to influence mortal minds. He can make entire armies do his bidding with a single thought!

**Gilgamesh**
The strongest Eternal is also the most kindhearted. He adores fellow Eternal Thena and cares for her through centuries of illness.

**Thena**
This acrobatic warrior can form any weapon out of cosmic energy. She lives with a mental illness called Mahd Wy'ry.

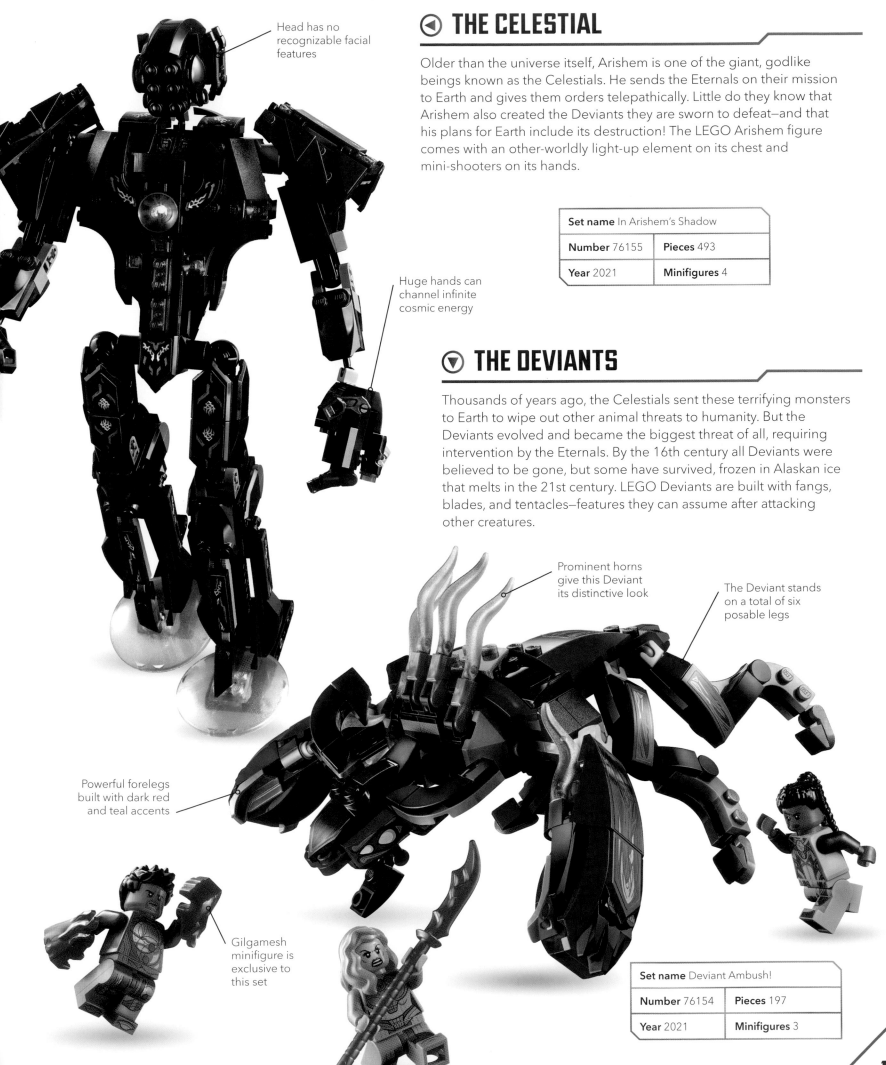

## ◁ THE CELESTIAL

Older than the universe itself, Arishem is one of the giant, godlike beings known as the Celestials. He sends the Eternals on their mission to Earth and gives them orders telepathically. Little do they know that Arishem also created the Deviants they are sworn to defeat—and that his plans for Earth include its destruction! The LEGO Arishem figure comes with an other-worldly light-up element on its chest and mini-shooters on its hands.

Head has no recognizable facial features

Huge hands can channel infinite cosmic energy

| Set name In Arishem's Shadow | |
|---|---|
| Number 76155 | Pieces 493 |
| Year 2021 | Minifigures 4 |

## ▽ THE DEVIANTS

Thousands of years ago, the Celestials sent these terrifying monsters to Earth to wipe out other animal threats to humanity. But the Deviants evolved and became the biggest threat of all, requiring intervention by the Eternals. By the 16th century all Deviants were believed to be gone, but some have survived, frozen in Alaskan ice that melts in the 21st century. LEGO Deviants are built with fangs, blades, and tentacles—features they can assume after attacking other creatures.

Prominent horns give this Deviant its distinctive look

The Deviant stands on a total of six posable legs

Powerful forelegs built with dark red and teal accents

Gilgamesh minifigure is exclusive to this set

| Set name Deviant Ambush! | |
|---|---|
| Number 76154 | Pieces 197 |
| Year 2021 | Minifigures 3 |

# SHANG-CHI AND THE LEGEND OF THE TEN RINGS

Shang-Chi and his best friend, Katy, live ordinary lives in San Francisco until they are targeted by The Ten Rings criminal gang. This forces Shang-Chi to admit to Katy that he was once a member of The Ten Rings—and that his dad, Wenwu, is the gang's immortal founder! Together with Shang-Chi's sister, Xialing, they seek out the mystical realm of Ta Lo, on a mission to stop Wenwu from unleashing an ancient evil.

Razor Fist's right arm in blade mode

Windshield gives Katy a clear view of the forest ahead

Bodywork is badly damaged en route to Ta Lo

Gang symbol is ten linked rings

| Set name | Escape from The Ten Rings | |
|---|---|---|
| Number | 76176 | Pieces | 321 |
| Year | 2021 | Minifigures | 4 |

## ⊙ JOURNEY TO TA LO

Shang-Chi and Katy make the perilous journey to Ta Lo in a car belonging to Ten Rings tough guy Razor Fist. They use the powerful 4x4 to escape The Ten Rings base, with Wenwu and his gang following close behind. The chase continues through a moving maze of trees and into the dimensional portal that links Earth to Ta Lo.

**Shang-Chi**
Wenwu raised his son to be a ruthless gang member, but Shang-Chi chooses to reject his father's ways.

**Katy**
Shang-Chi's best friend is a great driver but discovers her true destiny when she trains as a warrior in Ta Lo.

**Razor Fist**
This Ten Rings member is Wenwu's right-hand man—not least because he can turn his right hand into a scary sword!

## BRICK FACTS

A smaller—but still impressive—version of Ta Lo's resident dragon appears in the pocket-sized set Shang-Chi and The Great Protector (set 30454).

Dragon scales can be used to make strong armor

In times of great danger, Ta Lo is defended by a dragon known as the Great Protector. The dragon rises up from its underwater home to defend Ta Lo as it always has done. Both Shang-Chi and Xialing ride the Great Protector, which has a long, posable body, sharp claws, a spiky tail, and the ability to shoot LEGO water bursts.

Xialing clings to the creature's neck

Death Dealer fights with multi-pronged daggers

Wenwu wields the rings that give his gang its name

Long tail powers the dragon through air or water

**Wenwu**
The leader of The Ten Rings has lived for a thousand years, after finding ten mystical rings that grant him incredible powers.

**Xialing**
Like her brother, Shang-Chi, Xialing escapes from Wenwu in her teens. She teaches herself martial arts after Wenwu refuses to train her.

**Death Dealer**
This masked martial artist is one of Wenwu's meanest gang members. He trains the young Shang-Chi and treats him very badly.

| **Set name** Battle at the Ancient Village | |
| --- | --- |
| **Number** 76177 | **Pieces** 400 |
| **Year** 2021 | **Minifigures** 4 |

# THE X-MEN

The X-Men are a team of humans born with genetic mutations that give them extraordinary powers. Drawn from everyday communities around the world, they come together at Xavier's School for Gifted Youngsters in New York, where they learn to control their mutant abilities and use them as a force for good. Despite the team's name, the X-Men are not all men and have powers ranging from heightened senses and rapid healing to total control of the weather!

**Wolverine's mutant powers** grant him the keen senses of an animal, the ability to rapidly heal from injuries, and long retractable claws on both hands!

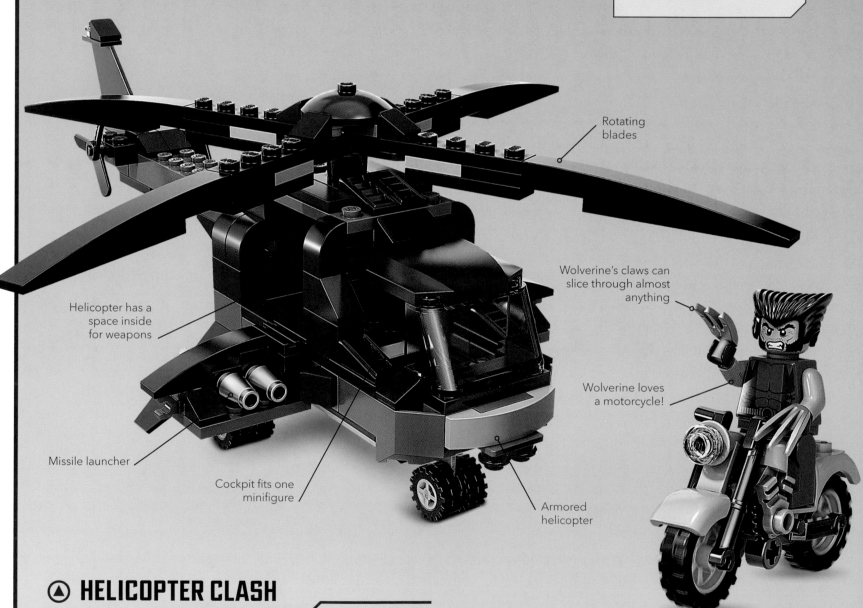

Rotating blades

Wolverine's claws can slice through almost anything

Helicopter has a space inside for weapons

Wolverine loves a motorcycle!

Missile launcher

Cockpit fits one minifigure

Armored helicopter

## ⓐ HELICOPTER CLASH

Wolverine faces numerous ruthless foes over the years, many with powerful weapons and tech, such as this missile-loaded helicopter. The chopper might have the advantage of flight, but Wolverine has enhanced durability, healing powers, and a speedy motorcycle, so perhaps it's a fair fight.

| Set name Wolverine's Chopper Showdown | |
|---|---|
| **Number** 6866 | **Pieces** 199 |
| **Year** 2012 | **Minifigures** 3 |

## ▶ STORMY BATTLE

Storm is one of the most powerful X-Men and sometimes leads the team. She can fly and create her own weather, generating blizzards, whirlwinds, lightning, and more. Storm can hold her own against most foes, even Magneto, the X-Men's most indomitable enemy. A fellow mutant with the power to control magnetic fields, Magneto believes that humans with special powers should rule over everyone else!

| Set name | X-Men Vs. The Sentinel | |
| --- | --- | --- |
| Number | 76022 | Pieces 336 |
| Year | 2014 | Minifigures 4 |

Storm fires lightning bolts from her hands

Magneto flies by levitating a metal platform

**Magneto's helmet** protects him from psychic attacks. It can be replaced with a white hair piece, which hints at his many years opposing the X-Men.

## ▶ SENTINEL ATTACK

The X-Men work to protect society, but some people are scared by their abilities and seek to wipe them out. Over the years, many villains have sent towering robots to track and capture mutants. These Sentinels can fly, have built-in energy weapons, and can detect mutants from afar. Wolverine's minifigure is captured by a towering Sentinel, but his X-Men teammates Storm and Cyclops are on their way to help!

Energy weapon built into wrist

Missile launcher

Rear compartment contains toolbox

Thrusters for flight

## ▶ THE BLACKBIRD

Also known as the X-Jet, the Blackbird is an advanced supersonic aircraft used by the X-Men. It is designed for vertical takeoff and landing and has room for a team of mutants. The LEGO version can fit four minifigures: two in the cockpit—one pilot, one gunner—and two in the rear, which can be accessed by opening the jet's roof.

Cyclops at the controls

**Cyclops's eyes** project beams that can blast through metal and even rock. Fortunately, his head piece includes the ruby-quartz visor that lets him control his optic energy.

# BUILDABLE FIGURES

These large-scale action heroes (and one villain) are designed to stand up to detailed and active recreations of epic Marvel moments. Buildable figures were among the very first LEGO® Marvel Super Heroes sets back in 2012, with three Avengers sets. The concept of buildable figures was revisited 10 years later, with a wider range of characters. Boasting many more pieces and extra height, these figures stand tall at 9in (24cm)—and even include a light-up Arc Reactor element for Iron Man!

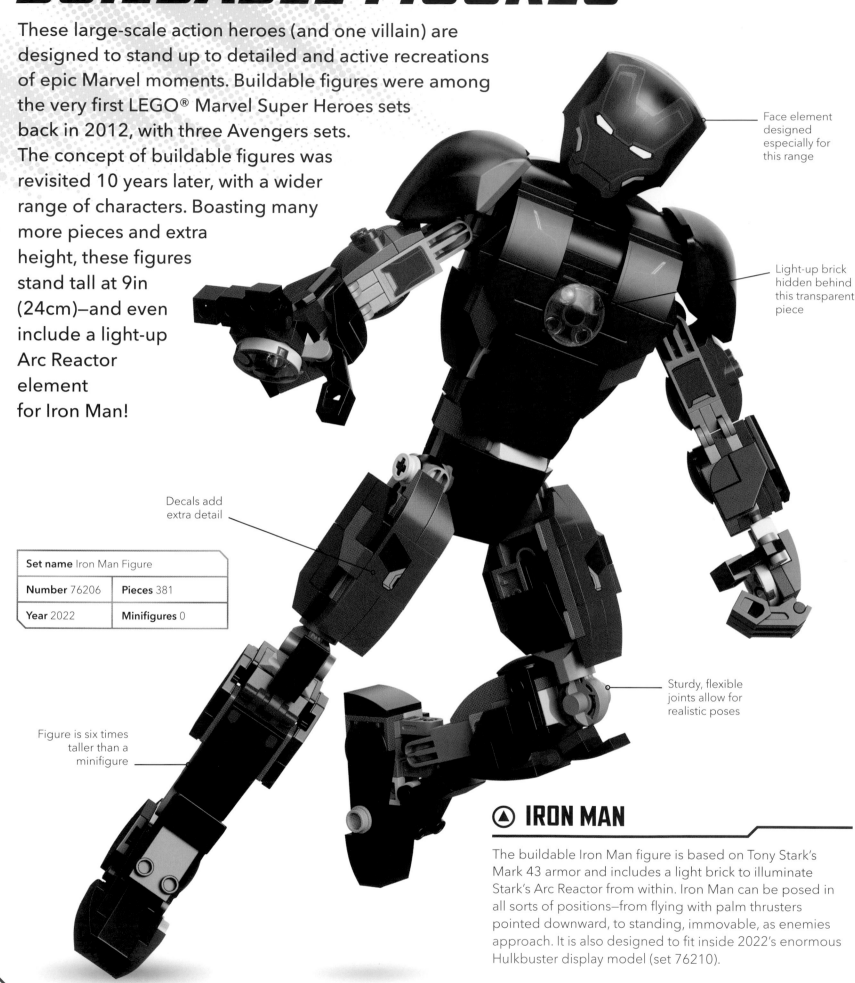

Face element designed especially for this range

Light-up brick hidden behind this transparent piece

Decals add extra detail

| Set name | Iron Man Figure | |
|---|---|---|
| **Number** 76206 | **Pieces** 381 | |
| **Year** 2022 | **Minifigures** 0 | |

Figure is six times taller than a minifigure

Sturdy, flexible joints allow for realistic poses

## ◭ IRON MAN

The buildable Iron Man figure is based on Tony Stark's Mark 43 armor and includes a light brick to illuminate Stark's Arc Reactor from within. Iron Man can be posed in all sorts of positions—from flying with palm thrusters pointed downward, to standing, immovable, as enemies approach. It is also designed to fit inside 2022's enormous Hulkbuster display model (set 76210).

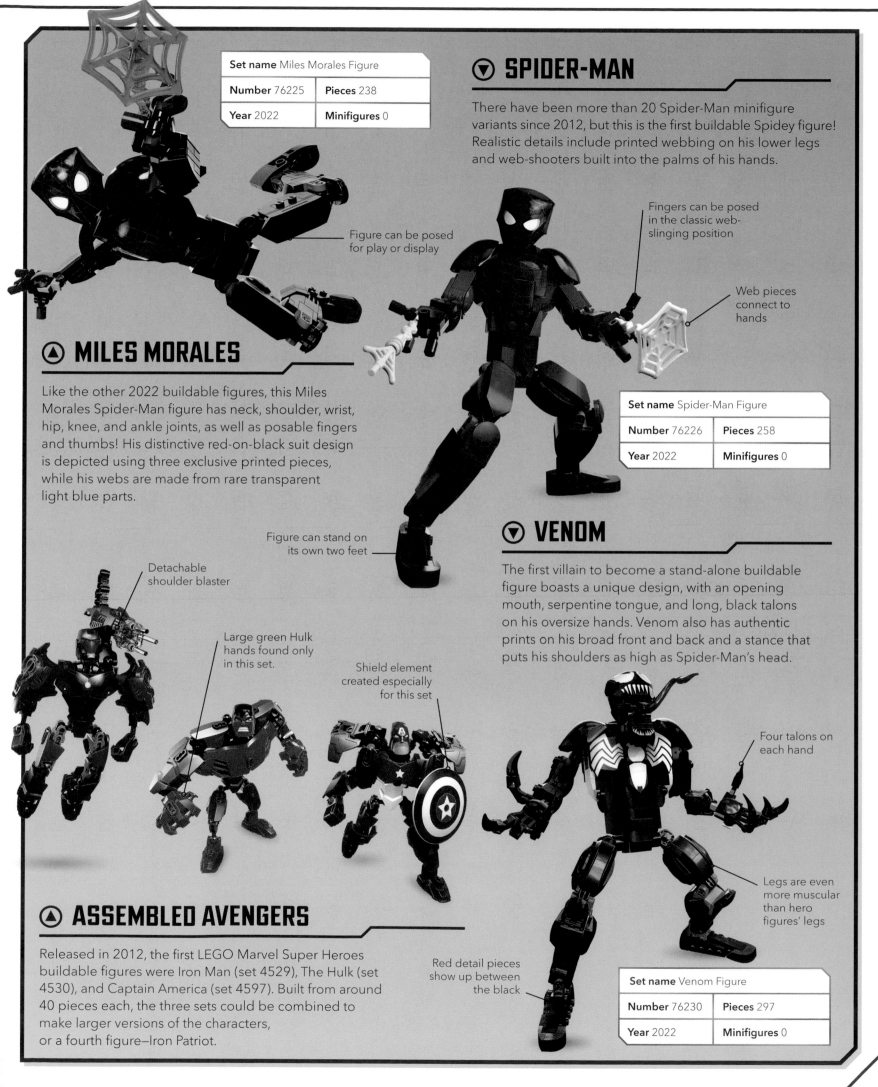

| Set name | Miles Morales Figure | |
|---|---|---|
| Number 76225 | Pieces 238 |
| Year 2022 | Minifigures 0 |

## ⊙ SPIDER-MAN

There have been more than 20 Spider-Man minifigure variants since 2012, but this is the first buildable Spidey figure! Realistic details include printed webbing on his lower legs and web-shooters built into the palms of his hands.

Figure can be posed for play or display

Fingers can be posed in the classic web-slinging position

Web pieces connect to hands

## ⊙ MILES MORALES

Like the other 2022 buildable figures, this Miles Morales Spider-Man figure has neck, shoulder, wrist, hip, knee, and ankle joints, as well as posable fingers and thumbs! His distinctive red-on-black suit design is depicted using three exclusive printed pieces, while his webs are made from rare transparent light blue parts.

Figure can stand on its own two feet

| Set name | Spider-Man Figure | |
|---|---|---|
| Number 76226 | Pieces 258 |
| Year 2022 | Minifigures 0 |

## ⊙ VENOM

The first villain to become a stand-alone buildable figure boasts a unique design, with an opening mouth, serpentine tongue, and long, black talons on his oversize hands. Venom also has authentic prints on his broad front and back and a stance that puts his shoulders as high as Spider-Man's head.

Detachable shoulder blaster

Large green Hulk hands found only in this set.

Shield element created especially for this set

Four talons on each hand

## ⊙ ASSEMBLED AVENGERS

Released in 2012, the first LEGO Marvel Super Heroes buildable figures were Iron Man (set 4529), The Hulk (set 4530), and Captain America (set 4597). Built from around 40 pieces each, the three sets could be combined to make larger versions of the characters, or a fourth figure—Iron Patriot.

Legs are even more muscular than hero figures' legs

Red detail pieces show up between the black

| Set name | Venom Figure | |
|---|---|---|
| Number 76230 | Pieces 297 |
| Year 2022 | Minifigures 0 |

# LEGO® BRICKHEADZ™

The LEGO Group debuted the first Brickheadz sets in 2016 as exclusives at San Diego Comic-Con. The small, buildable figures, characterized by their large heads, sit on a base and are meant to be easy to put together in one sitting. Iron Man is the Marvel character currently with the most Brickheadz designs. He was released as part of a duo set with Captain America in 2016, had a single release with a different design in 2017, and was released with Iron Man's Mark 50 armor in 2018.

**Rocket and Groot**
This duo set includes Rocket and Groot from Marvel Studios' *Avengers: Infinity War*. Groot comes with a video game accessory.

**Captain America**
Cap's iconic shield comes with the 2017 Captain America Brickheadz figure. It clips onto a stud on the back.

**Iron Man**
The 2017 Iron Man figure is the second Brickheadz version of Iron Man. It uses dark red bricks with dark yellow accents.

**Black Widow**
The Black Widow's realistic hairstyle, belt buckle, and baton accessories complete her iconic look.

**Hulk**
The Hulk Brickheadz wears his signature purple pants and includes a spiky hair build and printed-on muscles.

**Iron Man**
The Mark 50 Iron Man Brickheadz comes with more translucent blue bricks than previous versions, including within his armor and as his thrusters.

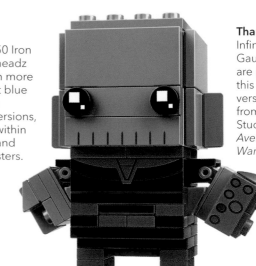

**Thanos**
Infinity Stone and Gauntlet details are printed on this Brickheadz version of Thanos from Marvel Studios' *Avengers: Infinity War*.

**Star-Lord**
Two detachable quad blasters are included with the Star-Lord 2018 Brickheadz figure, who also has red eye pieces and hair flowing over the top of his helmet.

## ▼ IRON MAN & CAP

One of the first Marvel Brickheadz sets was this pairing of Captain America and Iron Man. They depict the heroes' looks from the original *Marvel's The Avengers* movie. This set was a San Diego Comic-Con exclusive in 2016 and was available to purchase only by people who won a daily lottery.

**Gamora**
Gamora's pink-streaked hair adds some rare dark pink bricks to her Brickheadz figure. She also comes with a sword and wears her outfit from Marvel Studios' *Avengers: Infinity War*.

## ▼ SPIDEY & VENOM

The Spider-Man and Venom Brickheadz set was a 2017 San Diego Comic-Con exclusive. The 2017 Brickheadz sets expanded the baseplate from 4x6 to 6x6. Spider-Man has web printing on all four sides and comes with a white web string accessory. Venom's Brickheadz has enlarged eyes, four black tendrils, and a protruding red tongue.

## ▲ BLACK PANTHER & DOCTOR STRANGE

The Black Panther and Doctor Strange Brickheadz set was another 2016 San Diego Comic-Con exclusive. Both of these figures had printed necklaces, Black Panther's depicting his ceremonial tooth necklace and Doctor's Strange's showing the mystical Eye of Agamotto. Strange also comes with an energy shield on one of his hands.

# MIGHTY MICROS

The Mighty Micro sets were released between 2016 and 2018. Each set includes two minifigures and two vehicles—creating instant battle opportunities. The featured minifigures all have short legs so they can fit into the compact vehicles. Vehicles include cars, trucks, helicopters, and planes, most of which are themed to match their minifigure, and there are lots of unusual accessories to delight and amuse fans.

Pumpkin bomb

**The Spider-Man Vs. Green Goblin** set includes a Spidey copter-car and very green glider.

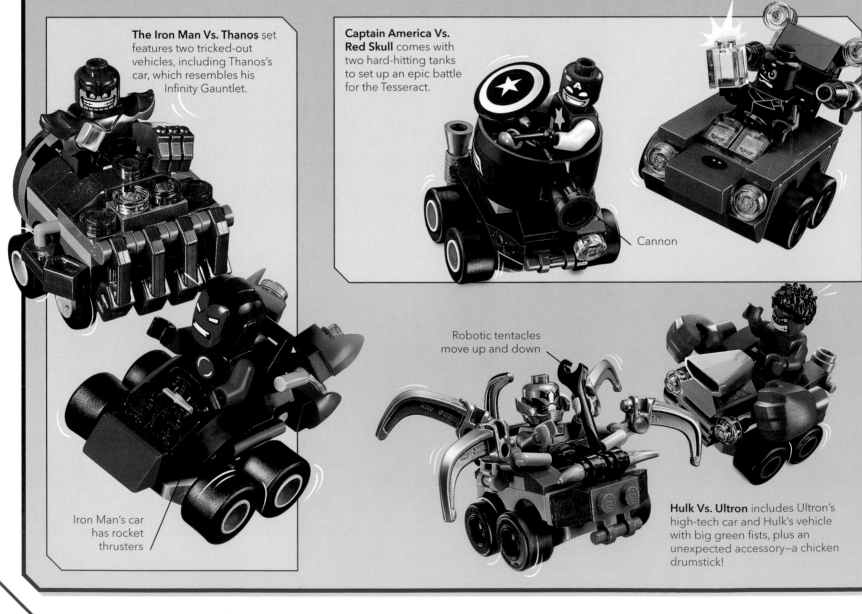

**The Iron Man Vs. Thanos** set features two tricked-out vehicles, including Thanos's car, which resembles his Infinity Gauntlet.

**Captain America Vs. Red Skull** comes with two hard-hitting tanks to set up an epic battle for the Tesseract.

Cannon

Iron Man's car has rocket thrusters

Robotic tentacles move up and down

**Hulk Vs. Ultron** includes Ultron's high-tech car and Hulk's vehicle with big green fists, plus an unexpected accessory—a chicken drumstick!

Magneto's magnetic power

**It's mutant versus mutant** in the Wolverine Vs. Magneto Mighty Micros set. Magneto's car is shaped around a large red magnet.

**The Spider-Man Vs. Scorpion** set comes with two animal accessories—a mini spider as well as a scorpion.

Scorpion's car has pincers

Wings can adjust

**It's Star-Lord versus Nebula** in this set. Will Star-Lord's Milano be able to catch Nebula's Necrocraft and take back his stolen cassette tape?

Transparent windshield

**There can be no mistaking** whose car is whose in the Thor Vs. Loki set. Thor's heavenly car has wings and lightning bolts, while Loki's has horns.

Sand loader full of sand

**Scarlet Spider** faces off against the Sandman in his speedy Spider Jet. Sandman drives a sand loader and holds a mallet made of sand.

# MECH SUITS

LEGO® Mech sets pair a minifigure with an armored mech suit for them to pilot. The minifigures fit inside the mechs' cockpits, which transforms them into a larger mech version of themselves. All of the mech builds are posable figures that can be articulated in a variety of ways, with gripping fingers and sturdy feet that enable them to stand on their own. The mechs feature super-sized characteristics and fun accessories of the characters they depict.

Spider chestplate

**76146: Spider-Man**

Shoulder stud shooter

**76140: Iron Man**

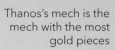

Thanos's mech is the mech with the most gold pieces

**76141: Thanos**

## ▲ 2020 MECHS

The Iron Man, Thanos, and Spider-Man mechs were all released in 2020. Iron Man's mech includes stud shooters and comes with a classic Iron Man minifigure. The Thanos mech comes with an imposing Infinity Gauntlet hand, with fingers waiting to snap. The Spider-Man mech has metallic spider arms sprouting from the back of the armor as well as a web with which to catch villains.

### MINI MECH

Spider-Man already had a small, mechlike vehicle before the big LEGO Mech sets came out. His Mini Spider Crawler (30451), released as a polybag in 2019, had eight legs, allowing Spidey to take the reins of a giant spider.

76168: Captain America

76169: Thor

Cape builds onto
the mech model

Mech stands at
4in (12cm) tall

76171: Miles Morales

## ▲ 2021 MECHS

In 2021, the LEGO Group released mech sets for
Captain America, Thor, and Miles Morales. Captain
America wields a giant shield and comes with a
unique Cap minifigure. Thor's hammer is similarly
large in his muscly mech, which includes a cape
as part of its armor design. The Miles
Morales mech comes with lots of
translucent electro-web accessories.

Extra-long
electro-web

76204: Black Panther

Claws made from
LEGO blade pieces

76202: Wolverine

## ▲ 2022 MECHS

The 2022 wave of Marvel mechs featured
Black Panther, Wolverine, and a new Iron Man. Black
Panther's mech has huge grasping claws and a high-
tech screen attachment. Wolverine's claws are made from large
blade pieces, giving his mech a fearsome look. The Iron Man mech
is very different from the 2020 mech and includes an energy shield,
palm stud shooter, and a unique Iron Man minifigure to fit inside.

76203: Iron Man

# COLLECTIBLE MINIFIGURES

In 2021, the LEGO Group released 12 unique Marvel minifigures that could be purchased only in mystery bags. The collectible minifigures come with display stands and a range of various accessories that include a Thor frog (Throg) and detailed laptop computer. The minifigures depict characters that feature in Marvel Studios' Disney+ streaming series, including *WandaVision*, *The Falcon and The Winter Soldier*, *Loki*, and *What If…?*

Cloak of Levitation references the team-up with Doctor Strange

Wings printed with Captain America colors

Shield covered in scuff marks

**Zombie Hunter Spidey**
A *What If…?* version of Spidey is on the hunt for a different kind of villain. He holds a string of white webbing with which to catch those zombies.

**Captain America**
Sam Wilson's new Captain America minifigure is printed with lots of red, white, and blue details. Silver highlights emphasize the stars and stripes, while the drone, Redwing, clips onto the back of the wings.

Tesseract

Tattered, dirty uniform

**Winter Soldier**
Bucky Barnes's minifigure is printed with his signature leather jacket and vibranium arm. He carries a dagger and Captain America's shield.

**Captain Carter**
Captain Carter appears in the *What If…?* series. Her minifigure wears a a crisp Union Jack uniform with sturdy brown boots.

**Zombie Captain America**
Captain America was among the Avengers infected by a zombie plague in a *What If…?* episode. His usually pristine minifigure is dirty and disheveled, and his skin is an eerie shade of blue.

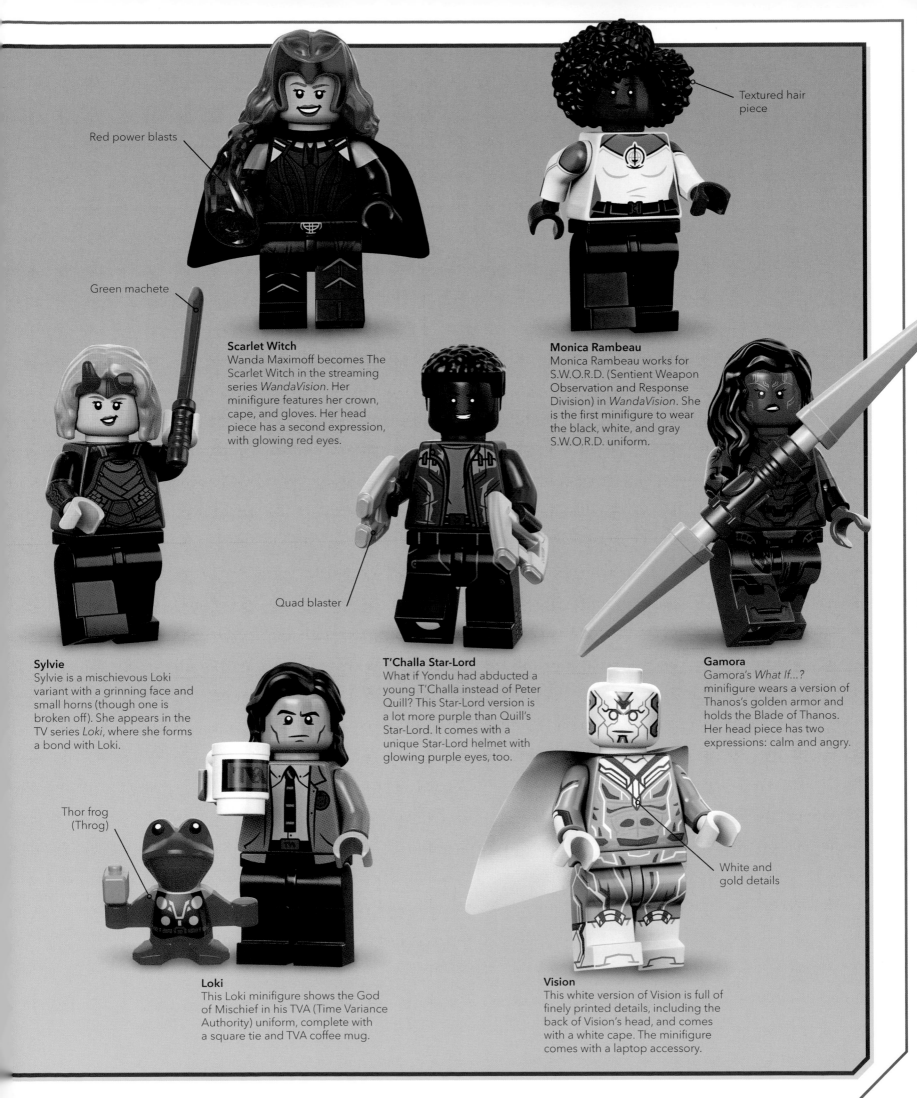

**Red power blasts**

**Green machete**

**Scarlet Witch**
Wanda Maximoff becomes The Scarlet Witch in the streaming series *WandaVision*. Her minifigure features her crown, cape, and gloves. Her head piece has a second expression, with glowing red eyes.

**Textured hair piece**

**Monica Rambeau**
Monica Rambeau works for S.W.O.R.D. (Sentient Weapon Observation and Response Division) in *WandaVision*. She is the first minifigure to wear the black, white, and gray S.W.O.R.D. uniform.

**Quad blaster**

**Sylvie**
Sylvie is a mischievous Loki variant with a grinning face and small horns (though one is broken off). She appears in the TV series *Loki*, where she forms a bond with Loki.

**T'Challa Star-Lord**
What if Yondu had abducted a young T'Challa instead of Peter Quill? This Star-Lord version is a lot more purple than Quill's Star-Lord. It comes with a unique Star-Lord helmet with glowing purple eyes, too.

**Gamora**
Gamora's *What If...?* minifigure wears a version of Thanos's golden armor and holds the Blade of Thanos. Her head piece has two expressions: calm and angry.

**Thor frog (Throg)**

**Loki**
This Loki minifigure shows the God of Mischief in his TVA (Time Variance Authority) uniform, complete with a square tie and TVA coffee mug.

**White and gold details**

**Vision**
This white version of Vision is full of finely printed details, including the back of Vision's head, and comes with a white cape. The minifigure comes with a laptop accessory.

# SCULPTURES

LEGO® sculptures focus on one character, accessory, or weapon and offer a complex and detailed model for builders to create. Released in 2021 and 2022, many of the LEGO Marvel sculpture sets come with display stands and nameplates that offer extra information about the characters or objects. Some come with minifigures, but not all. While these builds are meant to be displayed as sculptures, most of them can move or articulate into various poses, so there remains some element of play even once the build is complete.

| Set name Hulkbuster | |
| --- | --- |
| **Number** 76210 | **Pieces** 4,049 |
| **Year** 2022 | **Minifigures** 1 |

Head lifts up and chest opens to reveal cockpit

Light-up brick for palm thruster

Glow-in-the-dark piece

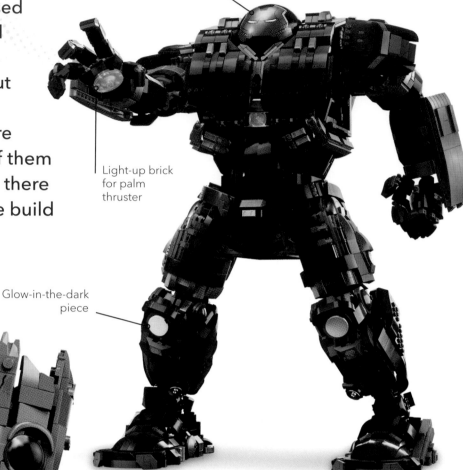

## ▶ GROOT

Groot can be one of the most unpredictable members of the Guardians of the Galaxy. But one thing Groot always makes time for is dancing—even if his fellow Guardians are busy tackling a monster or two during a job. LEGO builders can manipulate their Baby Groot sculpture into all kinds of dancing positions, and he even comes with a buildable version of Star-Lord's favorite cassette tape!

Printed tree details

| Set name I am Groot | |
| --- | --- |
| **Number** 76217 | **Pieces** 476 |
| **Year** 2022 | **Minifigures** 0 |

Twig elements

## ▲ HULKBUSTER

Tony Stark's Mark 44 Iron Man armor (also known as Hulkbuster) was created to help restrain the angry Hulk before Bruce Banner had full control over his alter ego. This substantial LEGO set contains more than 4,000 pieces and is big enough to live up to Hulk's massive standards at over 20in (52cm) tall. It includes light-up bricks, glow-in-the-dark bricks, and a Tony Stark minifigure in Mark 43 armor. The cockpit within this sculpture can fit the full Iron Man LEGO figure (set 76206) inside.

Decal with hand-written label

Awesome Mix vol.2

Realistic looking LEGO cassette tape

# INFINITY GAUNTLET

The Avengers face a formidable enemy in Thanos, who believes all worlds will benefit from losing half of their population. Thanos forces Eitri on Nidavellir to craft him an Infinity Gauntlet, a golden glove that can harness and channel the power of all six Infinity Stones. Thanos travels the universe collecting the stones until he uses the completed gauntlet to successfully remove half of the people in the world with a snap of his gauntlet-wearing fingers.

| Set name | Nano Gauntlet | |
|---|---|---|
| Number | 76223 | Pieces 675 |
| Year | 2022 | Minifigures 0 |

Includes all six Infinity Stones

A smooth build on the handle recreates the leather strap

| Set name | Thor's Hammer | |
|---|---|---|
| Number | 76209 | Pieces 979 |
| Year | 2022 | Minifigures 1 |

Jointed fingers can be articulated to form a snap

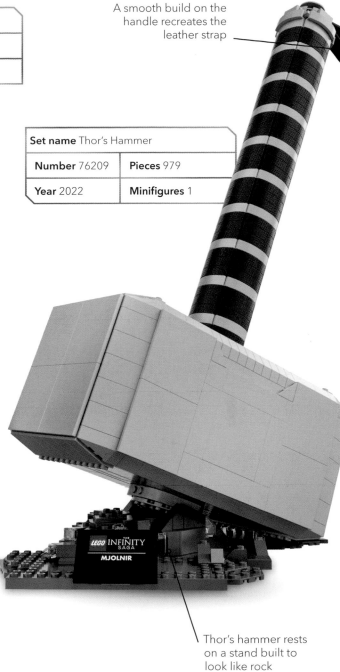

Thor's hammer rests on a stand built to look like rock

| Set name | Infinity Gauntlet | |
|---|---|---|
| Number | 76191 | Pieces 590 |
| Year | 2021 | Minifigures 0 |

## NANO GAUNTLET

Avenger geniuses Tony Stark, Bruce Banner, and Rocket work together using nanotechnology to create the Nano Gauntlet. The gauntlet is crafted to safely hold the six Infinity Stones so the Avengers can use them to undo the effects of Thanos's snap. While the gauntlet works perfectly, it is dangerous to wear because the stones emit gamma radiation.

## MJOLNIR

Mjolnir is Thor's hammer and one of his main weapons. It is a powerful combat weapon that can be wielded only by someone "worthy." Thor can summon Mjolnir from far away, use it to conjure lightning, and even use the hammer to fly. This sculpture is 18in (46cm) long, which is almost life-size! It features a secret compartment that can store a few accessories: a Thor minifigure, an Infinity Gauntlet, Odin's Fire, and a Tesseract.

# BUILDABLE BUSTS

Another type of LEGO sculpture that can bring Marvel to life is the character bust. These complex, fully 3-D LEGO sets focus on the heads and helmets of Super Heroes and Villains, including Black Panther, Iron Man, and Venom. Each bust contains hundreds of pieces, unique details, a display stand, and a nameplate. Creating these busts teaches new building techniques, which are employed to create a LEGO sculpture that is perfect from every angle.

## ▶ BLACK PANTHER

The Black Panther bust is the largest Marvel bust released so far. The build includes Black Panther's mask, necklace, and crossed hands. Based on T'Challa's look in Marvel Studios' *Black Panther* movie, the bust includes reflective silver detailing and background flashes of purple. Inside the bust is a design that forms LEGO pieces into the late *Black Panther* actor Chadwick Boseman's initials—which serve as a tribute to him.

Metallic silver details

Bust is 19in (46cm) tall

Fingers can articulate

Hands can detach from bust

Display base

| Set name Black Panther | |
|---|---|
| Number 76215 | Pieces 2,961 |
| Year 2022 | Minifigures 0 |

# IRON MAN

The Iron Man helmet was the first Marvel bust, released in 2020. The helmet features the iconic dark red and gold colors of many of Tony Stark's Iron Man armors. Stark created dozens of variations of Iron Man armor while he was an Avenger, including armor for James "Rhodey" Rhodes as War Machine and Pepper Potts as Rescue.

Eye sticker

| Set name | Iron Man Helmet | | |
|---|---|---|---|
| **Number** 76165 | | **Pieces** 480 | |
| **Year** 2020 | | **Minifigures** 0 | |

Nameplate

# VENOM

Venom is an alien symbiote that bonds with Spider-Man and later the journalist Eddie Brock. Venom is completely focused on taking down Spider-Man and has little control over his emotions. The alien has a black liquid form when it isn't using a host's body. This bust depicts Venom's scary features, incuding his monstrous teeth, unsettling grin, and long, red tongue.

Sharp teeth

| Set name | Venom | | |
|---|---|---|---|
| **Number** 76187 | | **Pieces** 565 | |
| **Year** 2021 | | **Minifigures** 0 | |

Decorative black printing

# CARNAGE

Carnage is the alien offspring of Venom. Also a symbiote, Carnage bonds with his hosts, offering them superhuman abilities. In many Marvel comics and Spider-Man movies, Carnage is a foe of Spider-Man and Venom. Carnage's most famous host was the murderous criminal Cletus Kasady.

| Set name | Carnage | | |
|---|---|---|---|
| **Number** 76199 | | **Pieces** 546 | |
| **Year** 2021 | | **Minifigures** 0 | |

Display stand

# EXCLUSIVES

Some LEGO® sets never hit store shelves and can only be acquired by being in the right place at the right time. And even then, you might need to have a bit of luck. Often, LEGO Marvel exclusives are giveaways or lottery-style prizes at conventions or special occasions. Many of these are minifigures that have not appeared in other other LEGO sets. A few LEGO Marvel exclusives have been larger sets featuring vehicles or even busts of characters.

Translucent bricks

## ▶ COMIC-CON ANT-MAN BUST SET

The promotional set at Comic-Con 2018 included a mini-bust of Ant-Man and a minifigure of Wasp, which, together, showed the two heroes at their relative sizes. Ant-Man's head can rotate in this bust, and his antennas move up and down.
The Wasp minifigure is not exclusive as she makes another appearance in Quantum Realm Explorers (set 76109).

Transparent wings

| Set name Ant-Man and the Wasp | |
|---|---|
| Number 75997 | Pieces 218 |
| Year 2018 | Minifigures 1 |

| Set name Rocket Raccoon's Warbird | |
|---|---|
| Number COMCON034-1 | Pieces 145 |
| Year 2014 | Minifigures 1 |

| Set name Throne of Ultron | |
|---|---|
| Number SDCC2015-1 | Pieces 203 |
| Year 2015 | Minifigures 4 |

## ▲ COMIC-CON ROCKET SET

A limited exclusive for Comic-Con 2014, some fans were lucky enough to purchase the Rocket Raccoon's Warbird set. It includes a version of Rocket in a maroon suit and a buildable Ravager ship that the bristly Guardian pilots to Xandar when Ronan the Accuser attacks.

## ▲ COMIC-CON ULTRON SET

The main villain of the 2015 Marvel Studios' *Avengers: Age of Ultron* film was featured in the 2015 Comic-Con LEGO set exclusive. Just 1,500 of the sets were sold, and they included four minifigures: Ultron and three sentries. Ultron's throne room is built on a 12x12 baseplate and uses columns, arches, and steps to depict his impressive seat in an old, dilapidated building.

The **2013 Comic-Con** exclusive was a Spider-Woman minifigure in a close-fitting red costume. This minifigure was given to approximately 350 fans.

# ⏫ TOY FAIR

There were 125 sets of unique Iron Man and Captain America minifigures given away at the 2012 New York Toy Fair. This Iron Man minifigure is unique as the only regular-size minifigure to have Iron Man's helmet printed directly onto the head piece. Some of these sets were also given away as prizes in a promotion for the LEGO Super Heroes Movie Maker App.

The **2015 Comic-Con** giveaway was an all-new Captain America (Sam Wilson) minifigure. On the packaging were the mysterious words, "Secret Wars."

This **2016 Comic-Con** giveaway is Captain America with a twist: This minifigure is from a Marvel Comics storyline where Cap secretly works for Hydra!

**Spider-Man** wears his advanced suit, featuring a large white spider on the front and back. This minifigure is from the Marvel Spider-Man PS4 video game, and was a giveaway at the 2019 Comic-Con.

# ⏫ COMIC-CON RAFFLE PRIZES

Minifigures of Jean Grey as Phoenix and a black symbiote version of Spider-Man were given to LEGO booth raffle winners during San Diego Comic-Con in 2012. The Jean Grey head piece can switch from a happier facial expression to an angrier one.

**Miles Morales** wears his classic Spider-Man suit in this minifigure from a Marvel PS5 video game. Released in 2020, it was a prize in a sweepstake that players had to beat the game to enter.

# ART SETS

LEGO® fans have more than one way to create. The LEGO® Art and LEGO® Brick Sketches™ sets are a unique way to build new versions of the legendary Marvel characters. Part jigsaw, part build-by-numbers, and part play, these sets include brick plates and LEGO pieces that form a design of recognizable shapes, characters, or 3-D forms. For Marvel, LEGO Designers created an art set for Iron Man and Brick Sketches portraits of Miles Morales and Iron Man.

Set comes with frame and hanging accessories

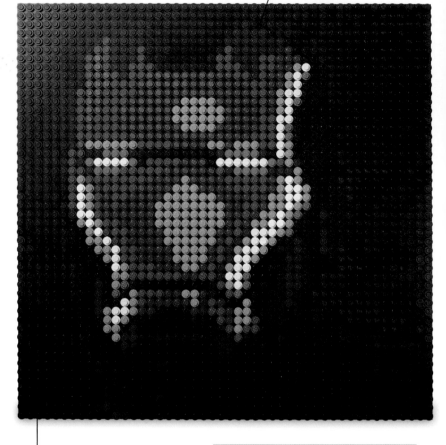

## ▶ IRON MAN ART

The Iron Man art set includes enough studs to create three different portraits of Iron Man: Iron Man in Mark 3 armor, Hulkbuster Mark 1, and Mark 85 armor. The portraits can be displayed individually on a shelf or wall, or all three sets can be combined to form the ultimate Iron Man portrait, which shows Iron Man holding out one of his repulsor gloves.

Thousands of studs are used to build up the picture

| Set name Marvel Studios Iron Man | |
|---|---|
| **Number** 31199 | **Pieces** 3,167 |
| **Year** 2021 | **Minifigures** 0 |

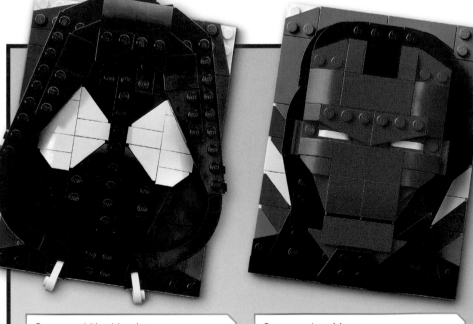

Built-in display stand

| Set name Miles Morales | |
|---|---|
| **Number** 40536 | **Pieces** 214 |
| **Year** 2022 | **Minifigures** 0 |

| Set name Iron Man | |
|---|---|
| **Number** 40535 | **Pieces** 200 |
| **Year** 2022 | **Minifigures** 0 |

## ◀ FACE FORMS

Younger LEGO builders can enjoy the LEGO Brick Sketches collection. Portraits of Miles Morales from Marvel Studios' movie *Spider-Man: Into the Spider-Verse* and Iron Man come with a 12x16 baseplate to create a 3-D artwork. The finished portrait measures 3x5in (8x13cm) and looks great on display!

# SEASONAL SETS

The first LEGO® advent calendar debuted in 1998, featuring 24 sealed boxes full of surprises—one for each day of the festive season. In 2021, the LEGO Group debuted the first Marvel advent calendar, with an Avengers theme. 2022 saw a Guardians of the Galaxy calendar. Each set comes with 24 small individual builds, which include several minifigures, many of which are dressed for holidays and unique to these sets!

Star-Lord on a holiday sleigh

## ▶ GUARDIANS ADVENT

The 2022 LEGO Marvel Advent Calendar has a Guardians of the Galaxy theme. Minifigures include Drax with a holiday sweater and Groot with a Christmas tree attached to his back. Other builds include a candy cane, a roasted turkey, and, of course, a cassette player.

| Set name Guardians of the Galaxy Advent Calendar | |
|---|---|
| Number 76231 | Pieces 268 |
| Year 2022 | Characters 6 |

Display each day's bricks and minifigures on the fold-out cover

This unique Nebula minifigure wears a Thanos and Infinity Stone themed holiday sweater.

Front flap folds down

## ◀ AVENGERS ADVENT

The 2021 version of the LEGO Marvel Advent Calendar includes Tony Stark in a holiday sweater, Black Widow with a marshmallow on the end of one of her batons, a gift-wrapping station, an Iron Man snowman, a Christmas tree, and a Thanos with a sack (full of presents, we hope)!

Thor wears a scarf and a cozy sweater on Day 22 of the 2021 Advent Calendar.

| Set name The Avengers Advent Calendar | |
|---|---|
| Number 76196 | Pieces 298 |
| Year 2021 | Minifigures 7 |

# SPIDEY AND FRIENDS

In the animated television series *Spidey and His Amazing Friends*, a young Peter Parker (Spider-Man), Miles Morales (Spin), and Gwen Stacy (Ghost-Spider) form Team Spidey as they work together to solve crimes. Team Spidey is joined by other young Super Heroes including Ms. Marvel, Hulk, Black Panther, and The Wasp as they take on villains including Rhino, Black Cat, Sandman, and Green Goblin. The TV series is popular among younger Spidey fans, so the LEGO Group released several sets that were easier for younger children to build.

## DUPLO® SPIDEY

LEGO® DUPLO® sets are made for very young builders. In Spider-Man Headquarters (set 10940), Spidey takes off on his chunky, single-piece blue motorcycle.

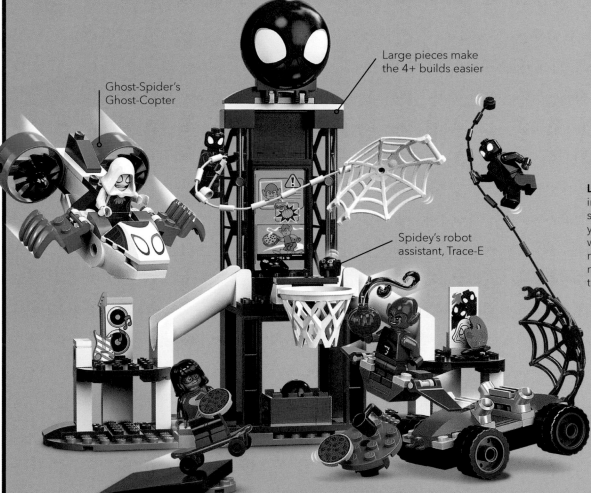

Ghost-Spider's Ghost-Copter

Large pieces make the 4+ builds easier

Spidey's robot assistant, Trace-E

**Like the other minifigures** in this set, Ms. Marvel has short legs. This gives her a younger look and, along with her printed blue mask and new hair piece, makes this version unique to this set.

| Set name | Spider-Man Webquarters Hangout | |
|---|---|---|
| **Number** 10784 | | **Pieces** 155 |
| **Year** 2022 | | **Minifigures** 5 |

## ▲ SPIDEY'S WEBQUARTERS

The Spider-Man Webquarters Hangout set is one of the LEGO Group's 4+ playsets, designed for preschool-aged builders. These sets come with a sturdy base, fewer pieces, and lots of minifigures and accessories. In Spider-Man's cool hangout he can play play guitar, eat pizza, paint a picture, or play a video game with Miles Morales, Ms. Marvel, and Ghost-Spider—or the young heroes can capture the Green Goblin in a colorful web trap.

**Doc Ock's mechanical** tentacles help her commit crimes. This minifigure wears red goggles and a green villain suit, and comes in the Spider-Man at Doc Ock's Lab set (10783).

# SPIDER-MAN 2003-4

The LEGO Group released several Spider-Man sets in 2003 and 2004 while the first two of Sam Raimi's *Spider-Man* films were playing in theaters. In addition to featuring minifigures of classic characters such as Spider-Man, Green Goblin, Doctor Octopus, and Aunt May, many of these sets feature Spider-Man taking on unnamed jewel thieves and criminals.

**This jewel thief** is up to no good in Spider-Man's Street Chase (set 4853). He is one of two thieves who steal a stash of LEGO diamonds. The minifigure sports a wild grin as he's chased through the streets by Spider-Man.

## BRICK FACTS

LEGO® Studios sets, such as Spider-Man Action Studio (set 1376), encourage brick builders to create stop-motion films using their LEGO sets.

## ◀ THE ORIGINS

This early Spider-Man set comes with two lab builds and a whopping six minifigures! Spider-Man's lab includes radioactive spiders in a glass box (and some that may have escaped), while Green Goblin's lab has a rotating chamber and lots of levers. Mary Jane and a generic scientist minifigure are included, as are two sets of alter egos: Spider-Man and Peter Parker, and Green Goblin and Norman Osborn.

| Set name Spider-Man and Green Goblin – The Origins | |
| --- | --- |
| **Number** 4851 | **Pieces** 212 |
| **Year** 2003 | **Minifigures** 6 |

**Norman Osborn,** also known as the Green Goblin, doesn't appear as his regular self in any other LEGO sets. His minifigure looks very different from his mean, green alter ego.

## ▶ VILLAIN'S HIDEOUT

This set also features minifigures of both Spider-Man and Peter Parker. Doc Ock's hideout on an abandoned pier houses a fusion machine and catapult. A speedboat provides the hero minifigures with a way to travel to the hideout, where they will find Doctor Octopus's minifigure as well as a potential hostage, Mary Jane.

| Set name Doc Ock's Hideout | |
| --- | --- |
| **Number** 4856 | **Pieces** 481 |
| **Year** 2004 | **Minifigures** 5 |

# Chapter 5: BEHIND THE SCENES

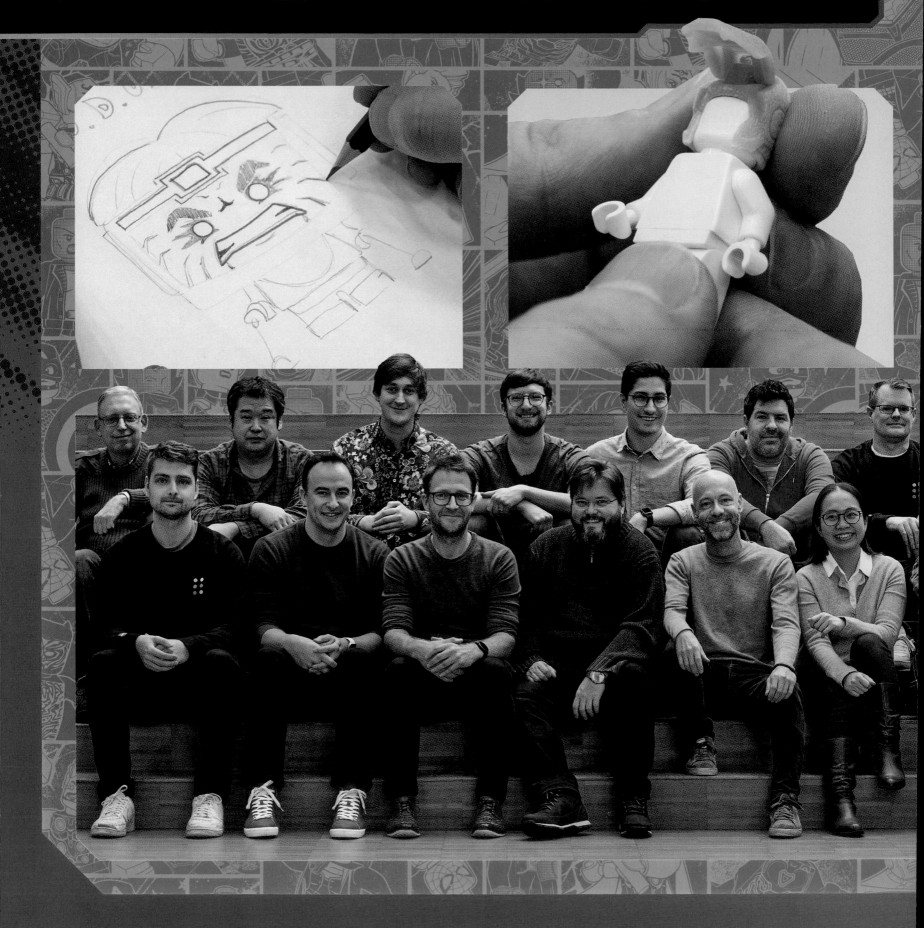

Back row, left to right: Bjarke Lykke Madsen, Model Designer; Junya Suzuki, Model Designer; Justin Ramsden, Model Designer; Chris Perron, Model Designer; Aaron Newman, Model Designer; Mark Tranter, Graphic Designer; Daniel Lundin, Graphic Designer; Tin Nguyen, Model Designer. Front row, left to right: Mathias Julin, Model Designer; Joel David Baker, Model Designer; Jesper C. Nielsen, Creative Lead; Mark John Stafford, Model Designer; Yoel Mazur, Element Designer; Thao Hoa Dinh, Production Lead; Adam Corbally, Associate Lead.

# Meet the team

It takes a squad of super heroes to bring each new LEGO® Marvel set to life. Their base is the LEGO Group headquarters in Billund, Denmark, and their mission is to make models and minifigures no Marvel fan can possibly resist! Here, the team reveal their not-so-secret identities, show off some builds from behind the scenes, share a few of their favorite designs to date, and much, much more...

## How many people does it take to make a LEGO® Marvel Super Heroes set?

JUSTIN RAMSDEN: Besides everyone you see here [see main image, above], there are also Element Designers, who create new pieces when we need them; Model Coaches, who make sure our builds are the best they can be; the people who create the building instructions; the Packaging Designers; and more. Without those real-life super heroes, there wouldn't be any LEGO Marvel Super Heroes sets! It's an immense collaboration, and just like the Avengers, we assemble to get things done!

**Helmet opens to reveal face print**

🔺 This exclusive Iron Man minifigure was designed by Agnieszka Ulatowska at the LEGO Group for this Visual Dictionary—the first LEGO Marvel book ever published! Iron Man is shown in unique armor that has a red-and-gold color scheme and comes with a front-opening helmet.

*"You can have any background to be a LEGO Designer, so long as you have the passion and imagination."*

*Mark Stafford*

# How do you land a dream job like a LEGO® Marvel Super Heroes Designer?

**MARK STAFFORD:** No two people have taken the same journey to get here. Some of us have come straight from university with design or engineering qualifications, and some of us were fan builders who turned our hobby into our job. You can have any background to be a LEGO Designer, so long as you have the passion and imagination.

**BJARKE LYKKE MADSEN:** I studied mechanical engineering, and now I have been designing LEGO sets in various different teams for more than 25 years! It really is a dream job.

**MARK STAFFORD:** It's not a dream job in this team, though—it's two dream jobs! One is getting to build LEGO sets for a living, and the other is getting to play with iconic Marvel characters all day.

**JOEL BAKER:** It's true. We sometimes joke about the fact that they keep sending us paychecks for coming in and playing with this stuff all day long!

**MARK STAFFORD:** Sssh! Don't give the game away!

## What's the best thing about the job?

**MARK STAFFORD:** For me, it's when we get photos and concept art from a movie that's currently being filmed. Getting to see those things before anybody else even knows they're in the movie is just incredibly exciting.

**JUSTIN RAMSDEN:** As we're fans, having each new movie spoiled for us two or three years in advance could easily be awful for us! However, Marvel always keeps some things super-secret and the plot points we do know about often end up changing, so it works out OK. Plus, by the time a movie does come out, we're so busy thinking about sets for future launches that we've probably forgotten what we were told about two years ago!

▲ These early concepts for the Sanctum Sanctorum (set 76218) depict it with an interdimensional portal made from flame pieces, and a rainbow-colored Bifrost bursting out of the roof! In the finished set, the portal is built without flames, and other features replace the Bifrost.

## And what are the biggest challenges that the job throws in your direction?

**JUSTIN RAMSDEN:** I think the biggest challenge with this theme—but also the beauty of it—is that you never know what you'll be working on next. One day you're an architect, then a spaceship designer. It's certainly never dull!

**JOEL BAKER:** It's also a challenge not to repeat ourselves. We always try to do something new—or to approach anything that's familiar in a different or surprising way. That leads to innovations like the Mighty Micros, the *Daily Bugle* [set 76178], and Thor's Hammer [set 76209].

**MARK STAFFORD:** For me, the real challenges are some of the shapes we have to recreate in LEGO form. When we find out that the Eternals have a triangular spaceship, or that the Guardians of the Galaxy's new ship is basically two hoops stuck together… Those are shapes we simply wouldn't attempt if we were creating a set on our own. Why would we do that to ourselves?! But when you see these amazing things that Marvel has created, that are going to look stunning on screen, it makes you raise your game.

**CHRIS PERRON:** When Marvel is designing a new spaceship, they don't have to imagine where a hand is going to grab it and swish it around… The challenge for us isn't just figuring out, "How do you build this?" It's "Where do you hold this?" and "How do you put it down flat on a table so that it doesn't break?"

**MARK STAFFORD:** Also, some things are so secret that Marvel can't tell us about them, however much they might want to. With *Spider-Man: No Way Home*, we didn't even know who the baddie was! But they want us to be able to do our job and come up with cool toys, so they let us invent a brand-new monster and put it in Doctor Strange's basement.

Add that sort of thing to the fact that we're often working to very tight schedules [because of movie release dates], and you can see why we have so manySenior Designers in this one team compared to some of the other teams in the building!

## How do you start creating a new set?

**JESPER C. NIELSEN:** It can start in different ways. When we are tying in to a movie that is in the process of being made, we talk to Marvel about what they think the iconic moments will be and what concept art or photos from filming that they can share with us. But our super-talented team is always noodling around with bricks, not always with a specific goal in mind. When one of those builds feels interesting, that starts a wider discussion and can end up becoming a set, without being based on a particular screen or comic-book adventure.

In part, I think that's what makes the theme so successful—finding that balance between representing cool movie moments and coming up with fun new ideas of our own.

**MARK STAFFORD:** There are also times when we come back to a movie after it has been released. I always enjoy that—when we know everything about a film and aren't just working from concept art and a rough story outline. In those cases, we start by looking at what we did before and thinking about how we can include more details, and focus on the moments in a movie that the fans really loved.

**ADAM CORBALLY:** One great example of that is the Quinjet. We designed the first one before *Marvel's The Avengers* came out, working entirely from concept art. We've returned to it in several sets since then, working from more detailed reference material each time. Our earliest Quinjets are still great to play with, but each new version is a bit more authentic than the last.

◀ These four versions of the Sanctum Sanctorum experiment with a four-story layout, different tree designs, different construction methods for the angled corner, and different positions on the 32x32 baseplate, among other variations.

The final, 2,708-piece version of the Sanctum Sanctorum, by Senior Model Designer Justin Ramsden, with Graphic Design by Adam Corbally, Daniel Lundin, Mark Tranter, and Ashwin Visser. ▶

*"When Marvel is designing a spaceship, they don't have to imagine how a hand is going to grab it!"*

Chris Perron

## Tell us more about those sets that are based on "noodling around with bricks"...

**JESPER C. NIELSEN:** When someone has a new idea for a vehicle, we ask ourselves, "Which character would make most sense with this vehicle?" Or if a Designer was working with a particular character in mind, we say, "OK, this vehicle is never going to appear in a film, but would it make some kind of sense if you found out it was being used just 'off camera'?" We do allow ourselves some leeway, because we want to make cool toys that you can play with. So, we don't worry about the fact that Spider-Man, say, doesn't traditionally rely on vehicles to get around. We start from the position that it would be fun if he did have some vehicles, and so, what should they be?

**BJARKE LYKKE MADSEN:** Those "homegrown" sets, as we call them, are my favorites for that reason. There are lots of cool characters we couldn't easily put into a LEGO set unless they came with a vehicle to build. So it's quite cool that we have this opportunity. If we think Spider-Man should have a giant, walking spider, Marvel is happy for us to make that happen!

Spider-Man's Spider Crawler (set 76114), designed by Bjarke Lykke Madsen with graphics by Mark Tranter and Tobey-Louise Brown, is an example of a set inspired by "noodling around with bricks" to see what happens.

## Is the design process done entirely with LEGO® bricks, digitally, or in other ways?

**CHRIS PERRON:** It varies from one Designer to another. I prefer working digitally right from the start, while other people want to get hands-on with bricks right away. The digital approach gives you every element at your fingertips, in the form of an on-screen, 3-D model. It also means you can work on things out of sequence—making parts float above others and filling in the gaps later on. Whichever way around you do it, though, eventually you will need both a physical model and a digital model working side by side.

**MARK STAFFORD:** Ninety-nine percent of what I do is hands-on with the physical bricks, but sometimes I'll start with a quick pencil sketch, just to identify the key features of a vehicle or whatever. Also, if we need a completely new part, I might sketch that and show it to the Element Designers, who will go away and turn it into something you can actually build with. They're great, and sometimes they will come back to you on the same day with a 3-D-printed part they've designed based on a simple doodle.

A concept sketch of Super Villain MODOK, as seen in Avengers: Hulk Lab Smash (set 76018) from 2014. This early design imagines MODOK with short minifigure legs, rather than the standard legs chosen for the final set design.

 3-D-printed parts such as this Iron Man helmet are not made from the same materials as real LEGO elements. They are designed only for short-term use.

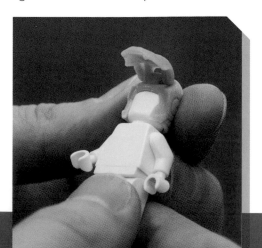

**ADAM CORBALLY:** Some of our Element Designers are old-school sculptors and will hand-craft new part prototypes from clay. It's awesome to see them work. Niels Milan Pedersen, who designed the first LEGO horse figure 40 years ago, still works here and he occasionally sculpts a Super Heroes part, which is just amazing to me.

**MARK TRANTER:** As a Graphic Designer, most of my work is done entirely digitally. In a theme that is so character driven, getting the minifigure design right is just as important as the model design, and doesn't necessarily involve getting hands-on with bricks at all!

## Which LEGO® Marvel Super Heroes minifigures have you most enjoyed working on?

**MARK TRANTER:** Two I really enjoyed are Iron Man Mark 1, from Iron Man Hall of Armor [set 76125], and Zombie Captain America [set 71031-9], from the 2021 collectible Minifigures series. With the first, I really enjoyed doing the layers—overlapping the panels to give it a real sense of depth and being pieced together from junk—and then adding scratches and damage and other metallic details. The second was fun because I got to design a Captain America suit, and then damage it with rips, holes, and dirt—even a bite taken out of the helmet! It's always fun to add some damage to a design.

▲ Sketches and prototype versions of the helmet worn by Captain America in LEGO Marvel Super Heroes sets since 2019. Mark Tranter modified this element's graphics for his Zombie Captain America design.

 Eight prototypes for Iron Man's helmet, and the finished element, far right.

▲ A prototype of the Cull Obsidian big figure, alongside the final design.

> "In a theme that is so character driven, minifigure design is just as important as model design."
>
> Mark Tranter

Early ideas for Super Hero Airport Battle (set 76051) captured in sketch form. This one sheet includes build concepts for the air traffic control tower, the baggage cart, and the Quinjet.

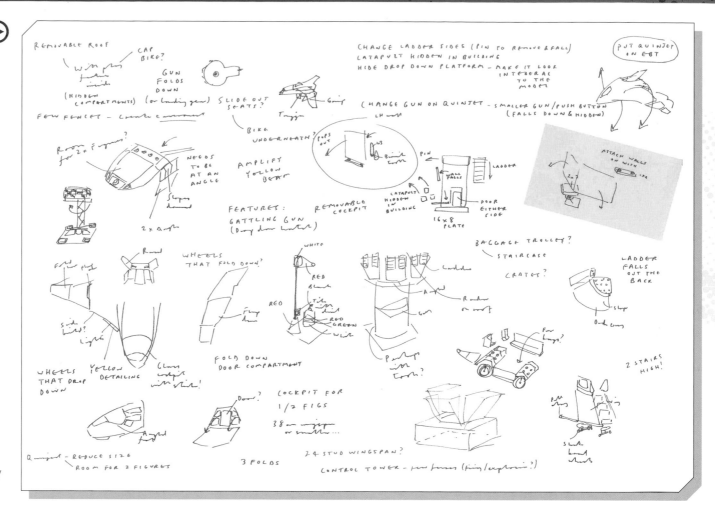

Senior Model Designer Justin Ramsden built many different versions of the Quinjet before arriving at the final design.

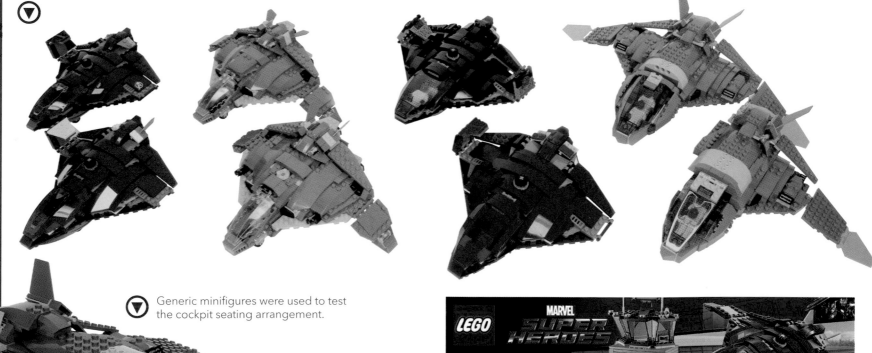

Generic minifigures were used to test the cockpit seating arrangement.

The finished set, with the addition of a Giant-Man figure created by Design Master Marcos Bessa. Graphic design for the whole set was by Adam Corbally and Casper Glahder.

"Itty-bitty Thanos" from the Mighty Micros range—a firm favorite of Senior Model Designer Joel Baker.

## What has been your favorite LEGO® Marvel Super Heroes set so far?

**MARK STAFFORD:** For me, it's 100 percent the *Daily Bugle* [set 76178]. I can't believe I got to make that! I came up with this sketch model, never believing it would be made into a real set. I started out with a list of about 75 Super Heroes that I loved, and I managed to get almost a third of them in there! Daredevil was always at the top of my list, because he is my favorite Super Hero and I've been buying the comic books since the 1980s. It's the set that allowed me to do everything I've ever wanted.

**JOEL BAKER:** It's a bit of an odd choice, but I've got to say Mighty Micros: Iron Man Vs. Thanos [set 76072], just because itty-bitty Thanos was absolutely hilarious.

**MARK TRANTER:** Of all the sets I've worked on, I would also say the *Bugle*. Of the ones I didn't work on, I think Thor's Hammer [set 76209] turned out really well. It's probably easier to pick favorites you didn't work on. How can you choose your favorite child?

**JUSTIN RAMSDEN:** I also find it very hard to choose favorites, but that's OK, because it's not our opinion that matters. So long as the fans find something to love in the sets we make, we must be doing something right.

**MARK STAFFORD:** Nah, it's definitely the *Bugle*, sorry!

## What is your one favorite feature in a LEGO Marvel Super Heroes set?

**ADAM CORBALLY:** Too many to list! There are loads that I love in Sanctum Sanctorum [set 76218] alone. The one I'll single out from that set is how Graphic Designer Ashwin Visser included the character of the Watcher in one of the interdimensional portals. If you haven't seen it or don't get the reference, it doesn't spoil your enjoyment of the set at all. But if you do, it's a little extra win.

**BJARKE LYKKE MADSEN:** I love the power blast elements we have introduced to physically represent super-powers. For me, they are one of the cornerstones of the theme. You can see them on the box fronts and might think they were a special effect, but then you find they are elements you can put into the minifigures' hands and use in different ways, and not have to imagine the powers out of thin air.

**MARK TRANTER:** I like that you can only pick up Thor's Hammer if you're worthy. How did they do that?

Spot The Watcher, top left in this detailed set graphic.

A Captain Marvel minifigure with power blast elements.

## What dream LEGO Marvel Super Heroes set do you hope to make one day?

**MARK STAFFORD:** I can't say, because then it won't happen. It has to be a surprise, and I'm hopeful that it really will happen one day. I'll tell you when it comes out!

**JOEL BAKER:** I think we should do the Hulk's shorts—at life size! We've done Iron Man's Nano Gauntlet and Thor's Hammer… It's only fair that the Hulk gets some ragged purple shorts.

**MARK TRANTER:** How about a wearable Iron Man suit?

**EVERYONE ELSE:** Yes!

# INDEX

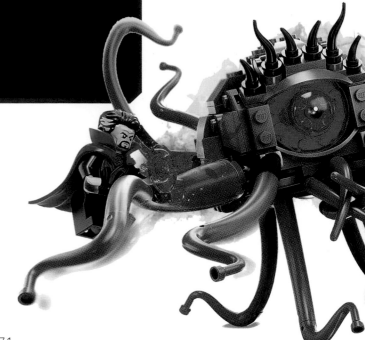

**Senior Editors** Laura Palosuo and Shari Last
**Designers** James McKeag and LS Design: Sadie Thomas,
Rhys Thomas, Samantha Richiardi, and Tory Gordon-Harris
**Senior Production Editor** Jennifer Murray
**Senior Production Controller** Lloyd Robertson
**Managing Editor** Paula Regan
**Managing Art Editor** Jo Connor
**Publishing Director** Mark Searle
**Jacket Designer** James McKeag

DK would like to thank Randi K. Sørensen, Ashley Blais,
Heidi K. Jensen, Martin Leighton Lindhardt, and
Adam Corbally, Justin Ramsden, and the rest of the
LEGO Marvel Super Heroes Design team at the LEGO Group;
Chelsea Alon at Disney Publishing; Caitlin O'Connell at Marvel
Comics and Kristy Amornkul, Sarah Beers, Capri Ciulla, and
Jacqueline Ryan-Rudolph at Marvel Studios; and, at DK,
Matt Jones, Julia March, and Tori Kosara for editorial help
and Jennette ElNagger for proofreading.

First American Edition, 2023
Published in the United States by DK Publishing
1745 Broadway, 20th Floor, New York, NY 10019

Page design copyright © 2023 Dorling Kindersley Limited
DK, a Division of Penguin Random House LLC
23 24 25 26 27  10 9 8 7 6 5 4 3 2 1
001–335739–Sep/23

DK books are available at special discounts when purchased
in bulk for sales promotions, premiums, fund-raising,
or educational use.
For details, contact: DK Publishing Special Markets,
1745 Broadway, 20th Floor, New York, NY 10019
SpecialSales@dk.com

Printed and bound in China

**For the curious**
**www.dk.com**
**www.LEGO.com**

MIX
Paper | Supporting
responsible forestry
FSC™ C018179

This book was made with Forest
Stewardship Council ™ certified
paper – one small step in DK's
commitment to a sustainable future.
**For more information go to
www.dk.com/our-green-pledge**

Join now and unlock a world of unbelievable benefits and
rewards. Scan here or sign up now at **LEGO.com/VIP**